FLORENCE SCOVEL SHINN'S

Guide
Life TO

**Harness the Power of Intuition,
Connect to the Laws of Attraction,
and Discover Your Divine Plan**

Sarah Billington

Published by:
Ulysses Press
PO Box 3440
Berkeley, CA 94703
www.ulyssespress.com

ISBN: 978-1-64604-312-5
Library of Congress Control Number: 2021946577

Printed in the United States by Kingery Printing Company
10 9 8 7 6 5 4 3 2 1

Acquisitions editor: Claire Sielaff
Managing editor: Claire Chun
Editor: Renee Rutledge
Proofreader: Barbara Schultz
Front cover design: Ashley Prine
Interior design and layout: Jake Flaherty
Artwork: cover © chasiki/shutterstock.com; interior © Gregor
   Buir/shutterstock.com
Production assistant: Yesenia Garcia-Lopez

Contents

> "Every man has power to lift the fog in his life. It may be a fog of lack of money, love, happiness, or health."
>
> —Florence Scovel Shinn,
> *Your Word Is Your Wand*

I will also investigate the differences and surprising similarities between organized religion and spirituality/agnosticism (page 14), and between prayer and the practice of manifestation (page 16).

Through reading this book, you will learn how and why to trust your intuition (page 20), and how your subconscious, conscious, and superconscious minds influence your beliefs and work together to affect your whole life. You will learn tips and tricks on how to adjust those beliefs to help you be more content, peaceful, and prosperous.

You will also discover the benefits of practicing affirmations, how they work, and how to recite them for the most effective results. You will come to understand how expressing gratitude can change your entire life for the better (page 51), and learn how to be conscious of a Divine Plan for your life that you may not currently be aware of (page 56).

Following a discussion of the many laws of the Universe, with examples and case studies showing them in action, over one hundred affirmations will be broken down into categories to get you started manifesting and attracting your dream life into being (page 63).

After reading this book you will be armed with all the tools you need to begin harnessing the power of the Universe, changing your mindset, and transforming your life. Even if you don't believe that the Universe has a plan for you, by repeating positive thinking and gratitude, you can truly change your outlook on life and attract happiness.

Though the benefits of self-improvement, positive thinking, and mindfulness are well recognized today, in 1925, when fifty-four-year-old New Jersey native Florence Scovel Shinn first discussed these concepts in *The Game of Life and How to Play* It, she was absolutely a woman ahead of her time.

With strong faith in God and her background as a teacher of metaphysical theory and New Thought teamed with an accessible and easy-to-understand teaching style, Florence became a thought leader in the metaphysical space. Many of her philosophies are just as relevant today as they were in the early decades of the twentieth century, if not more so.

So, who was Florence Scovel Shinn anyway, and what did she teach?

CHAPTER 1

Who Was Florence Scovel Shinn?

If you were to mention her name, many people these days would ask, "Who is Florence Scovel Shinn?" So, you may be surprised at the lasting impact this children's book author and illustrator turned New Thought leader has had on millions of individuals and groups around the world to this day.

Born September 24, 1871, in Camden, New Jersey, to Emily Scovel (née Hopkinson) and Alden Cortlandt Scovel, a practicing lawyer, Florence was the middle child between an older sister and younger brother. Being educated himself, it is no surprise that Alden encouraged Florence's own education.

Florence grew up to be a freethinking woman in an America changed by the women's rights movement of the 1840s, but long before the first American woman would be granted the right to vote. She attended the Friends Central School, then studied art at the Pennsylvania Academy of Fine

Arts from 1889 to 1897. Here she also met her future husband, painter of impressionistic and realistic works, Everett Shinn.

Together, Florence and Everett moved to the Washington Square area in New York City. He found success in painting and writing theater shows. She, meanwhile, was not content as a lady of leisure or housewife as was typical for women of the time, but worked as an illustrator of popular children's literature in magazines and books. Her illustrations were a perfect snapshot of late-nineteenth and early-twentieth century horse-drawn carriages and lamp posts, of top hats and dapper daywear.

In 1912, after fourteen years of marriage in a time when divorce was rare and very much taboo, all was not well between the married couple, and Everett requested a divorce from Florence.

As a divorcée living in New York City, Florence was a shining example of women emerging from the patriarchal lifestyles enforced by prior generations, an example for future generations that women could be more than just wives and mothers if they wanted.

After living through the Great Depression and devastation of World War I, Florence went on to believe, even after witnessing and experiencing such loss, that anyone, even a woman, could manifest their own destiny if they believed in it enough. And so she did. Florence grew to be a well-known and well-respected metaphysics thought leader in her time, holding salons and private sessions with clients in need of guidance, as well as writing books and positive affirmations in the early to mid-1900s. The concepts of metaphysics that Florence studied, taught, and consulted on in the first half of the twentieth century, then known as New Thought, are more commonly known today as the Law of Attraction and the ideas of manifestation, affirmations, and positive thinking.

In 1925, at fifty-six years old, after failing to secure a publisher for her book of metaphysical theory, Florence took action and self-published *The Game of Life and How to Play It*. The book has left its mark on today's most influential thought leaders the world over, such as motivational author Louise Hay, Rhonda Byrne, creator of the documentary *The Secret*, and Tony Robbins, a leader in the personal development and success training space.

Florence's writing is unpretentious and accessible and, though the book's language is charming in its dated tone, it still holds up for modern readers today. In it, she grounds metaphysical theories with hundreds of examples from her own life, the lives of others she encountered, and comparisons to Bible verses, opening the laws of the Universe to readers of any faith or lack thereof.

Florence Scovel Shinn's successful book was followed by *Your Word Is Your Wand* (1928), *The Secret Door to Success* (1940), and a posthumously published collection of her seminars and talks, *The Power of the Spoken Word* (1945). Her lasting legacy is a prime example of the laws of the Universe in action; she maintained faith that God would provide for her, overcame obstacles and rejection, and followed the Divine Plan of her life, and as can be seen by her impact on the world and lasting legacy, she was rewarded for it.

CHAPTER 2

What Are Metaphysics and Metaphysical Theory?

Metaphysics, from the Greek words *meta ta physika*, meaning "after the things of nature," is the philosophy that an important aspect of reality exists and affects us from outside of what we can perceive with our physical senses in the physical world. We are attuned to a change in the atmosphere, for example, but this attunement has nothing to do with sight, touch, smell, hearing, or taste. But we are certain it exists, all the same.

You can't touch Wi-Fi, but its signal is all around you in most cities and beyond, powering our world.

You can't sense bacteria or viruses in your body, but your body may eventually begin to react to their presence within you.

You can't feel the pressure of gravity, but it holds you close to the Earth and prevents you from floating away into space.

These are all forms of energy that we can't experience through our five senses but still acknowledge. Energy is all around us, making changes to the world and affecting our own lives.

The laws of the Universe are exactly the same; they are energy forces that impact our lives though we cannot actively sense them around us.

Perhaps something happened and without looking at the person next to you, you know what they think about it. You can feel the energy shift, or you know without a shadow of doubt that you are thinking the exact same thing. Or, think of a time you entered a room immediately after an argument and the atmosphere felt heavy, oppressive, and even dangerous. The hostility lingered in the air between the warring parties. The negative energy impacted how your body felt, as you became tense, on alert, or may have wanted to leave the room again. You may have decided not to be in a room alone with those people again. Their thoughts and reaction to each other, or the situation and the resultant energy they gave off, changed the environment and maybe even your behavior.

Your thoughts and your energy are more powerful than you know, causing fundamental changes to your life and that of others, and therefore, the world. You can harness that energy to create the life of your dreams. You can't touch, taste, see, smell, or hear that change in the environment, but the energy will affect you anyway.

How Metaphysics and Religion Coexist

There are generally three types of people: those who follow an organized religion (see page 13), those who are agnostic, or spiritual while believing the existence of God or other ultimate realities is unknowable (see page 14), and those who are atheist and don't believe there is a higher power guiding us at all. Many classify themselves as one of these three and believe there is generally no overlap in between. But you may be surprised at how spirituality and the word of God in Bible Scriptures overlap.

In *The Game of Life and How to Play It*, Florence discusses both the law of God and the laws of the Universe, often adding "(law)" to the end of Bible quotations when talking about the power of God, so closely does she connect belief in guidance from God with belief in guidance from the Universe.

In making the law of God and the laws of the Universe interchangeable, Florence's books filled with Bible verses and Scripture can also easily provide instruction on how to live well for spiritual people, highlighting their understanding of what the Universe provides. Belief in a higher power, whatever form that may be, is all it takes.

Florence's teachings show there is much more in common than it seems between those who have faith in organized religion and worship one or more deities, and those who are spiritual, with the belief that there is something with good intentions toward us in the Universe we don't understand that is pulling the strings.

The laws of God and the laws of the Universe are so similar, in fact, that people who follow each will likely have very similar principles and philosophies about how to live a good life.

Both organized religion and metaphysics encourage surrender of the ego and personal pursuits and maintain that, with focus and acceptance, God, or the Universe, will provide what is right for you, whatever that may be, and it might not be what you expect.

Examples of concepts and rules to obey in organized religion that are also found in metaphysics and the laws of the Universe include:

+ "You reap what you sow" from the Bible is the same sentiment as the Law of Karma (page 82) in metaphysics, that if you do bad, bad will happen to you.

+ "Condemn not lest ye also be condemned" from the Bible is the sentiment behind the Law of Attraction (page 70), that whatever thoughts and actions you put out into the Universe you will attract more of those same thoughts and actions back to you.

As I'll cover in a bit more detail in the next section, religious and spiritual people hold the common belief that something all-powerful is pulling the strings, is in control, and has a plan for them that they don't know about, but whether this higher power is a deity or a source of energy is where their conclusions differ. On the other hand, those who are atheist do not believe in a higher power guiding us through life. Rather, they believe they, the circumstances they are in, and the society they are a part of are solely responsible for their lot in life. They take full responsibility for their failures and their successes, believing their prosperity or lack thereof to be solely of their own making.

Differing Beliefs

Organized Religion

Those who are religious believe in and worship a God, or some form of supernatural being, that acts through conscious thought and makes decisions that impact every individual's life and the planet for better or worse. If you are religious, you have a system of religious attitudes, beliefs, and practices and commit your life to serving your God. You are someone who lives with thanks to a God for your blessings; follows God's guidance from the Bible (or other appropriate book of faith) for living a moral and good life; and prays to your God. Those with faith in a God believe He or She nudges them gently toward learning opportunities and their destiny, or away from that which could harm them.

Spirituality/Agnosticism

Those who consider themselves spiritual or agnostic don't believe there is a person actively listening to their prayers and pushing them in one direction over another. But they do feel *something greater than themselves* is at work, that they are connected to it, but that they may not have nailed down exactly what it is. When you're in the right place at the right time—and you usually would not have been there—spiritual people believe that is the Universe guiding you.

Those who consider themselves spiritual believe the Universe itself, not an entity like God, Jesus, Krishna, Buddha, or Allah conspires to provide for them. Like those who practice organized religion, they have faith in a Divine Plan for their lives that they may not know about.

People do not typically consider themselves both religious and spiritual. If you believe in a God (or many), you can consider yourself spiritual in terms of that belief, but generally not in terms of the Universe at large assisting you.

There is no right or wrong way to be spiritual, however. Take what feels right to you from any religious or spiritual practice and live your life according to your own faith and beliefs.

CHAPTER 3

Prayer or Manifestation? There Is No Right or Wrong

For those who practice a religious lifestyle and worship a God, prayer is the act of speaking to God about the blessings they dream of for themselves or for others, and it is a moment to thank Him or Her for the life and blessings they have been provided.

Those who are spiritual and don't believe in a personified higher power express their wishes to the Universe all the same. However, instead of praying to a specific God, they practice manifestation.

*"Therefore I tell you, whatever you ask in prayer,
believe that you have received it, and it will be yours."*
—Mark 11:24

This quote from the Gospel of Mark mirrors an important cornerstone in the art of manifestation, showing a clear link between faith in organized religion and spirituality.

As Jesus said to "believe that you have received [whatever you ask for], and it will be yours," metaphysical manifestation of your desires encourages gratitude for having already been granted what you desire and, through your visualization and belief that it is true, the Universe brings more of it toward you.

The practices of prayer and manifestation assist you to live a happy and peaceful life.

What Is Manifestation, and How Do You Do It?

The practice of manifestation is a cornerstone of metaphysical theory and attracting your desires toward you. You don't need to surround yourself with crystals or sit cross-legged with the sounds of soothing ocean waves lapping the shore, or a gentle breeze rustling through the leaves of a peaceful forest. You don't need to be in the meditative zone to manifest, but you do need to take a moment, wherever you are, to be present and focus inward.

You can practice manifesting anywhere at all: while commuting in the car, sitting on the sidelines at your child's swim meet, over a coffee break, out for an evening stroll, in the quiet moments in bed before you get up for the day, or heck, maybe in the bath or shower. Any time you can take a couple of minutes to yourself and focus inward on your dreams and goals is the perfect time to practice manifestation.

Manifestation often comes in the form of affirmations, either repeated aloud, silently to yourself, or in written form. Try to use all your senses and focus on what you want and how you'll feel when it's yours. Will you feel butterflies in your stomach and warm all over in a new, loving relationship? Will stress melt away to a sense of pride and achievement at a business success or financial windfall? What will your dream change for the better in your life? Hold that image—that feeling—and focus on it. Believe that it is real. And don't limit your dreams! Stay open, even to possibilities that are beyond your wildest dreams and what you think you need. You could do a lot of good with excess, so do not shy away from dreaming big. And then dream bigger still.

Remember to Let Go

Focus on your desires so that you attract them to you, but at the same time, don't hold onto them too tightly. Florence advises that you're not in control, here; God, or the Universe is, and it knows what is best for you.

For example, if you focus too hard on a specific goal, like your offer on a specific house you love being accepted, you might successfully manifest that into reality, and you could very well live happily there, but there may have been a different house in another town that the Universe had planned for you. Another house where you would have moved next door to a person who would have gone on to make a dramatic, life-changing impact on your future, who you may never meet if you focused on manifesting that other house that you wanted but was not meant for you.

Let go of the need to control your life, and trust that the Universe has your back. You may not always get what you want, but sometimes, even when you can't see any other way, what you think you need is not what you truly need to reach your dreams. The real way forward isn't going to be a straight line; it's going to be twisty, and it might surprise you. But have faith in the journey. Just let go.

CHAPTER 4

Your Secret Power Within: Intuition

"Intuition means, in-tuition, or
to be taught from within."

—FLORENCE SCOVEL SHINN,
The Game of Life and How to Play It

Intuition.

That gut feeling.

A hunch.

Sometimes you just *know* you are on the right path, or you may sense that the opportunity before you, as amazing as it looks on paper, *feels* wrong. You could perceive an internal alarm when you meet someone or have a hunch that there's something just a little bit off about that dark street. Or maybe, the business you started isn't successful but you just know if you don't give up, eventually, it will be.

Have you ever had a gut feeling about something but gone against it? You knew the trivia answer but told yourself it didn't sound right, so you answered with your second thought. But your first thought was correct. This happens constantly in my own life, and I'm sure it happens to you too. Your intuition knows the correct answer or the right path and is infinitely more knowledgeable than your logical, conscious brain that second-guesses and thinks the situation through to the wrong conclusion.

When your intuition is telling you something, there is often no outward evidence as to whether it's right or wrong. But sometimes, deep inside, your body simply knows. This is what Florence calls "your secret power within; your secret magic." Because no one else has the same intuition as you, as no one's journey is the same. What is right for you may not be right for someone else.

Is It Intuition or Guidance?

Some people stop trusting their intuition. They rely on outward facts and data to help them make their decisions, so their gut feeling about particular situations starts to soften. It gets quieter as the conscious brain takes over their decision-making. But your conscious, logical brain doesn't have all the answers. It may be trying to make decisions without all the necessary information. For example, imagine you have been tasked with bringing a plate to the office morning tea, and you decide to bring something sweet. Will you bring doughnuts or a fruit salad? You choose the refreshing fruit salad as a healthy option as you know some of your colleagues are calorie-conscious. Fruit salad it is!

But wait, you remember an amazing doughnut place near the office with custom fillings and flavors. Bringing those doughnuts would be a huge hit! Who really wants a fruit salad compared to those delectable doughnuts? You decide to bring the doughnuts. They're obviously the better option.

However, if you had known that three of your colleagues also anticipated what a hit the doughnuts would be and would choose to bring them to morning tea, would you maybe have stuck with your intuition that you should bring the fruit salad (which was sorely missed at the staff gathering on a table full of doughnuts)? With so many pastries, the fruit salad would have been the huge hit and standout dish with your peers.

> "Intuition is a spiritual faculty and does not
> explain, but simply points the way."
> —Florence Scovel Shinn,
> *The Game of Life and How to Play It*

A Definite Lead

Sometimes your intuition will be strong and speak to you powerfully. You will feel it in your nerves, in your muscles, down your spine, and in your heart that the choice is clear; this is surely the right way, you don't know how you know but *you know*.

Or, you could intuit that this is most definitely the *wrong* way. You will feel it in the sick feeling in your stomach and the tightness in your chest.

But then, other times, your intuition might be quieter, or you can't feel it at all through your confusion as to what decision is the right one.

This is when Florence says to ask the Universe for a definite lead.

Sometimes we get a feeling, a hunch that tells us to accept what we may usually have declined; for example, we have an overwhelming desire to visit the bakery when we don't commonly eat pastries; or we make a last-minute decision to stop off at a store on the way home.

Don't ignore these powerful urges, especially when they're unusual for you. Keep your eyes open and pay attention to your intuition.

But I Don't Like This Bakery

Florence herself once had a sudden urge to visit a bakery a couple of blocks away. She didn't want anything there but decided to go anyway. When she arrived, she perused the breads, pastries, and delicious goods, but she had been right: there was nothing she particularly wanted.

On her way out the door, Florence ran into a woman she had known a long time before and had thought of recently, a woman who was in need of and very grateful for Florence's guidance. She had not been drawn to the bakery for baked goods, after all.

"Often, one goes for one thing and finds another," Florence says, which is exactly what happened when she felt that overwhelming feeling within—her intuitive lead—that she should visit the bakery, not later, but right then.

CHAPTER 5

Conscious, Subconscious, and Superconscious

It's easy to think we walk around making well-thought-out decisions and taking deliberate action, but as the study of psychology proves, a lot more goes into who we are, how we think, and what we do than you might realize. While most people know about the conscious and subconscious, many have not heard of the superconscious. All three minds shape our thoughts and, in different ways, impact how we live. The more you understand them, the more you can control them and change your life in unfathomable ways.

The Conscious Mind

Your conscious mind is your active brain. It interacts with the world around you. It processes the experiences of your five senses and tells you not to touch something when it's hot, or that something that smells bad may not be safe to eat.

Your conscious is active throughout your waking hours, processing and helping you through your daily life using reasoning and logic and thinking through repercussions to actions.

It's where you weigh up pros and cons and ponder what to do next, which direction to turn, whether to order the beef or tofu stir-fry—a million small decisions that, like a butterfly flapping its wings in Australia causing a hurricane in Hawaii, combine to shape the whole of your day, your week, your life.

Should I take the freeway or the back streets home?

I'm too tired for the gym tonight so I'll skip it. Again.

I can't stop thinking about how much I hate them.

One more beer won't kill me.

Will I accept the job offer?

Should I say "I do, 'til death do us part"?

Every conscious decision can have far-reaching consequences and potentially change the direction of your life.

Skipping exercise every day will have an effect on your health, one more beer is fine unless you decide to drive home or are mentally incapacitated with your guard down among others who may wish you harm.

Marrying that person and committing to them might be the best decision you ever made, or be short-sighted and foolish and lead to a life of misery for you both.

But what is driving your decisions? Where are they coming from?

The Subconscious Mind

"The subconscious, being simply power without direction, carries out orders without questioning."
—Florence Scovel Shinn, *The Game of Life and How to Play It*

We talk about our subconscious thoughts and opinions, but how much do you really know about the effect your subconscious thoughts have on the way you interact with the world and go about your life? How much does your subconscious affect how you see yourself? Deep down, your abilities, your worth, what you have to contribute to the world, and your relationships heavily impact the decisions your conscious mind makes, big or small, from minute to minute. And how you feel about yourself and others, at its core, lives in the depths of your subconscious.

For example, you may have dreams of stardom, as many do, or of becoming an award-winning actor, recognized by your peers and fans and monetarily compensated for your immense talent as a thespian. But something stops you from auditioning or promoting yourself. Perhaps deep in your subconscious, no matter how much you want it, you don't truly believe in yourself, your acting ability, or your worthiness of the success and recognition you desire.

Another example can be difficult for many to confront: you may not think you have a racist bone in your body, but sometimes, your actions prove differently, and over the years, through the media you have consumed and the individual experiences you have had, you may have developed some subconscious biases you are not consciously aware of. But these can be changed.

Florence writes of the subconscious:

"Every thought, every word is impressed upon it and carried out in amazing detail. It is like a singer making a record on the sensitive disc of the phonographic plate. Every note and tone of the singer's voice is registered. If he coughs or hesitates, it is registered also. So let us break all the old bad records in the subconscious mind, the records of our lives which we do not wish to keep, and make new and beautiful ones."

The laws of the Universe and the process of manifesting and affirmations (page 63) can help you reprogram your subconscious beliefs to align with and help you toward your desires and a happier life.

Case Study
The Poor Body Image Ripple Effect

Anita looks in the mirror and doesn't like what she sees. She pinches the fat on her belly; she frowns hopelessly at the acne popping up on her face, at the frizziness of her hair. She's single and lonely. She longs to be in a loving relationship but won't put herself out there and go on dates because who would love her the way she is now? She is ashamed of her body fat and her skin. She declines invitations to parties because she doesn't want to be embarrassed, to be ignored because of how hideous she is. Even if she did meet someone nice, there's no way she would be good enough for them. Everyone is out of her league.

She couldn't possibly go and exercise at a gym or park and face the potential mortification of being ridiculed or laughed at as she huffs and puffs while she works on bettering her health.

Full of self-loathing, Anita's conscious mind is in pain but without quite understanding why. She soothes herself by sitting in front of the television where it's safe and no one could hurt her, eating ice cream, which is sweet and delicious and makes her feel good.

Anita's subconscious thoughts about herself, that she is too big and ugly and not worthy of love, that if she attends a party with strangers or works out in a public place she will be ridiculed and hurt, greatly impact the decisions her conscious mind make. To skip the party. To go to the gym tomorrow. That it's way more fun to watch TV by herself tonight. Her subconscious beliefs about herself are telling her that the world is a scary place and people are cruel to those who look like her, which is not necessarily the case at all.

But what if Anita didn't have these feelings about her body and self-worth? What if, when Anita looked in the mirror and touched her soft skin, she shrugged? It's just her body. Everyone has some fat on them. What if she didn't focus on her size so much because she is so much more than that? If she saw the pimples on her skin and sighed with annoyance but didn't let it define her? Everyone gets acne sometimes, even adults. She's not the only person to have a blemish or scar. If Anita believed, deep down to her core, in her subconscious, that she was more than the sum of her looks, how might that change the decisions she might make with her conscious mind about attending a party or going to the gym?

Imagine Anita believing that she is quick-witted and people would laugh at her jokes and enjoy being around her. She believes that she's killing it at work and feels a sense of pride in her accomplishments. Would she worry that people would ignore her—or worse—ridicule her at a social event? That any potential partner or even potential friend she met would be out of her league? Hell, no! She'd attend that party with enthusiasm because she knows she has a lot to offer.

She could form closer bonds with old friends, make connections with new ones, or even find a potential partner at the party, which she certainly couldn't do alone from her couch at home.

Anita wouldn't feel the need to comfort eat and hide away from the world and, in turn, would be ingesting fewer calories.

The only difference between the two Anitas is how she feels about herself, and that subconscious belief about herself has greatly impacted the decisions her conscious mind makes and, consequently, the evolution of her life.

What her subconscious believes comes into being.

Limiting beliefs that emanate from the subconscious around applying for a new job, particularly when attempting to take a step up, or into a new career path, are also very common.

"I'm not qualified enough for that job," you might say to yourself upon reading a job listing for a position that makes you excited. Or perhaps, "I've always dreamed of starting a business, but what if I'm a failure? It's better to stick to my dead-end job where it's safe and secure." Yes, starting a business is difficult, and you could fail.

But what if you didn't? We talk ourselves out of possibilities before we even try.

A hard lesson learned across the globe throughout the COVID-19 pandemic has been that even the most secure jobs can become insecure in the blink of an eye. We assumed people will always need to travel for business or pleasure, that there would never be a time when restaurants wouldn't be needed and gyms wouldn't be essential because fitness is important for human health. They're secure industries, aren't they?

Sure, until the world shut down, closed borders, and canceled flights and gatherings. The pandemic proved that staying in your secure, safe job instead of taking a risk and following your dreams may not be as secure as you think. So if the lackluster job you've been in for a long time could be just as insecure as taking a chance on something new that you're passionate about, but your limiting beliefs convince you is too risky, why not try anyway?

Here's another example of the subconscious mind driving limiting beliefs: the person you're in a relationship with is okay; you're not particularly happy, but it's fine. They want to marry you. Would you even find anyone else who would marry you if you didn't say yes? It's easier to stay than it is to strike out alone. You're not good on your own, so you'd better say yes.

And another: learning to paint can take a long time and a lot of practice, and you might be bad at it. But what if you're amazing?

Don't allow your subconsciously held thoughts about yourself, your place in the world, your abilities, or your self-worth be negative ones. Don't allow your subconscious thoughts to sabotage you before you even set foot on the starting line.

> *"Man's soul is his subconscious mind, and*
> *whatever he feels deeply, good or bad, is*
> *outpictured by that faithful servant."*

—Florence Scovel Shinn, *The Game of Life and How to Play It*

How Can You Change Your Subconscious Thoughts?

Subconscious thoughts are below your conscious thoughts. You don't even know what they are so how are you supposed to change them?

There are very simple ways to change your subconscious thoughts. Anyone is capable of these techniques, and you can do them at any time. It takes practice and perseverance but can make a world of difference in how you feel about yourself and others, and you can find them right in this book in Chapter 7: What Are Affirmations, and How Do They Work? (page 40) and Chapter 8: The Power of Gratitude (page 51).

The Superconscious Mind

The superconscious, Florence says, is "the Christ within" and is the crucial part of you that focuses on forgiveness. Christ, as a principle, is within every one of us. Working with the conscious and subconscious, it carries the weight of taking our sins away and bearing our burdens. When we forgive ourselves for the wrong we have done, the superconscious takes the weight of that burden so that you may still live your life with peace.

The superconscious, the Christ within, is the person made in God's image, likeness, and love.

"All big ideas meet with opposition."
—Florence Scovel Shinn, *The Secret Door to Success*

Just as many a performer experiences stage fright and cannot make themselves take the stage, oftentimes we meet with opposition and roadblocks to achieving our wildest dreams. Often the biggest roadblock isn't external. It's not someone else saying no—it's you saying no to yourself. Your own doubts, worries, insecurities, and fears rejecting you before you can be rejected by the world, before you can fail. We are each our own biggest opposition.

Florence writes:

> "There is a place that you are to fill and no one else can fill, something you are to do, which no one else can do. There is a perfect picture of this in the superconscious mind. It usually flashes across the conscious as an unattainable ideal—something 'too good to be true.'
>
> In reality it is man's true destiny (or destination) flashed to him from the Infinite Intelligence which is within himself."

This is the superconscious at work, guided by the subconscious, which is simply power with no direction. The superconscious is where creativity lies, forgiveness can be given and received; it is the realm of perfect ideas.

Take note of those "too good to be true" notions that may flash through your conscious mind, as they may very well be a path worth investigating to set you on the way to even your wildest dreams.

CHAPTER 6

Expectancy

"The horse-shoe or rabbit's foot contains no power, but man's spoken word and belief that it will bring good luck creates expectancy in the subconscious mind, and attracts a 'lucky situation.'"

—Florence Scovel Shinn,
The Game of Life and How to Play It

Florence knew two people who were prime examples of the power of your expectation.

"I always miss a car," (I assume this to mean public transport, a trolley car, or tram) the man she knew said. "It invariably pulls out just as I arrive."

Whereas his daughter said to Florence: "I always catch a car. It's sure to come just as I get there."

Deep down, in his subconscious, the man expected a bad outcome: the car would just be leaving—infinitely worse than it not being in sight at all—and he was rewarded with that annoyance again and again. His subconscious believed what he told it and therefore brought more of that experience. His daughter, on the other hand, expected a favorable outcome, that the car would always arrive just as she needed it and would get her where she was going on time, and she received exactly that.

There is no logical reason why he missed every car, unless his clock was permanently behind, or why she caught them all. But their expectations could have impacted their success (or lack thereof).

Just like people who believe they are intrinsically lucky expect things to work out in their favor in the end, in a big or small way, often they are indeed lucky. And those who believe they are unlucky and expect the worst often find this belief confirmed as misfortune and the worst outcome inevitably happens.

It's Not the Lucky Rabbit's Foot Bringing You Luck

Four-leaf clovers, horseshoes, rabbit's feet—this odd selection of items and others like them are considered to be "lucky." On the flip side, black cats and walking under ladders are supposed to bring bad luck.

But having the object isn't what brings the good or bad luck toward you. It's what you believe about it and what you expect will happen because of having it in your possession that is making all the difference. Florence cautions against the worship of icons through the following recollection:

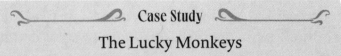

Case Study
The Lucky Monkeys

In *The Game of Life*, Florence wrote of two men she knew: "Two men in my class had had great success in business for several months, when suddenly everything "went to smash." We tried to analyze the situation, and I found, instead of making their affirmations and looking to God for success and prosperity, they had each bought a "lucky monkey."

I said: 'Oh I see, you have been trusting in the lucky monkeys instead of God.'"

"Put away the lucky monkeys and call on the Law of Forgiveness," she told them, explaining that man has the power to call on the Law of Forgiveness and neutralize his mistakes. Placing their trust in the hands of the monkeys, and not God, the Universe, or even themselves, was most definitely a mistake.

The two men decided to rid themselves of the "lucky" monkeys entirely, and all went well for them again.

Just because the two men chose to rid themselves of their lucky charms entirely and found success again afterward doesn't mean you need to discard your own lucky charm. If you want to, keep it as a reminder, a talisman, that you expect luck and good fortune, but remember that the object doesn't hold the power, the Universe does. The only thing a lucky object does is give you that feeling of expectancy of good things to come.

It can be a vicious cycle: you expect bad luck so your subconscious attracts more bad luck, thus confirming to you that you are unlucky. Consequently, you continue to expect it.

But you can break this cycle and retrain your subconscious to attract luck, peace, prosperity, love, happiness, or whatever else you desire by changing your expectations. And one way to do this is through affirmations.

CHAPTER 7

What Are Affirmations, and How Do They Work?

> "Ask, and it shall be given you, seek, and ye shall find, knock, and it shall be opened unto you."
>
> —MATTHEW 7:7

A world of joy, abundance, and prosperity wait out there for you, but as Jesus is quoted in Matthew 7:7, man must make the first move. No one can bless you with what you desire, not even the Universe, if you don't ask for it and no one knows you want it. That's where affirmations come in.

If you have never heard of affirmations, or have but always thought they're woo-woo, hippie-dippie stuff, then you'd be surprised to know you have used affirmations in your own life without realizing it. Consider the following affirmations, for example:

I can do it.

I've got what it takes.

Everything is going to be okay.

At their essence, affirmations are positive phrases or statements used to challenge negative or unhelpful thoughts. With regular practice they can vastly change the way you think, how you feel, and how you go about your life.

During challenging times, such as in the midst of a heavy workload or during a crisis, such as a breakup or perhaps a traffic accident, "I can do it," "I've got what it takes," and "Everything is going to be okay," are common sayings you might say to yourself. Instead of freaking out and dwelling on how much work there is and how little time you have, whether anyone will ever love you again, or how you are going to afford a new car and get around, you might pause, break the cycle of negative thoughts, and tell yourself:

"It's going to be okay."

"I can get through this."

"I have what it takes."

And then say it again.

These are simple affirmations, personal pep talks if you will, that change your mindset, boost your self-confidence, and help set you on the path to success.

By telling yourself that you have what it takes, you will begin to act like someone who has what it takes. Instead of getting overwhelmed, feeling defeated, and giving up in a pit of despair, you're more likely to work through possible solutions and try something, because you can get through this. And if you believe that, and keep trying, then everything will be okay.

The more you tell yourself positive things—that you are capable, that good things are coming—the more you'll believe these things and the more confident you will feel that you have what you need for everything to turn out okay. Alternatively, if you spend your time dwelling on negative thoughts and telling yourself that you can't do it—that you have social anxiety, for example, or that you are unlovable—then you are more likely to believe it and, in turn, stop trying because you are confident you cannot do the thing. You'll stop attending parties because you become too anxious, and you'll close off your body language and stop noticing people who are attracted to you.

How Affirmations Train Your Brain: Habit-Forming Repetition

The more you do something, the better at it you become. But why is that? Let's break this down. Write your name somewhere, right now (just humor me). How does it look? Pretty much the same as it has since you finished learning to write in grade school? What hand do you write with? And how long have you been writing with that hand? Decades?

Now, write your name with your nondominant hand. What is your handwriting like with that hand? Not as neat, right? A bit of a mess, even? Your brain has had years and years of repetition writing with your dominant hand, so it has formed shortcuts, quick pathways between your synapses in your brain and your dominant hand in how to write your name. Because you have not repeated the habit of writing with your nondominant hand, your brain has not formed those pathways, and it doesn't work as well. It's never going to be as neat unless you practice. You would have to do it again and again. Then repeat.

Just as we learn to write, or dance, or drive, or do anything in our lives through repetition, the exact same behavior can—and does—have a drastic impact on how you see the world and yourself and live your life.

You are learning and becoming an expert at whatever behaviors you repeat. If you repeatedly tell yourself that you are not good enough, then your brain is getting a lot of practice in believing that you are not good enough. And if you believe you're not, then you will act as if you aren't. You won't try, you won't apply, you will convince yourself that whatever it is simply is not for you.

Doors won't be shut on you, you'll be shutting those doors yourself.

Let's go back to your handwriting. When was the last time you wrote something, like notes to yourself, a letter, or a grocery list by hand? Has it been a while? Living in the digital age, most of us communicate more through typing on devices or with our voices than handwriting these days. If this is you (it's certainly me!) and it's been a long time since you wrote something down by hand, what did your name look like when you wrote it? Even with your dominant hand, was your handwriting a bit sloppier than it used to be? Are you a bit out of practice, maybe?

Decide to use affirmations and tell yourself you can do it—that you're qualified and capable, that going to the gym each day makes you feel energized and strong, or that you're ready to love someone and be loved again— instead of telling yourself that you can't. As you become better at telling yourself you are worthy, you will become worse at telling yourself that you are not.

Future-Tense vs. Present-Tense Affirmations

Florence encouraged others not to speak in future tense when stating their affirmations and attracting their desires toward themselves, but to speak in present tense. It is a subtle but infinitely important difference.

Saying "everything I want will come to me" is full of hope. You are thinking positively. But have you ever felt a bit stressed about something and told yourself it will be okay, only to feel that niggling hint of doubt wriggling around in the back of your brain, not quite squashed by your hopeful, affirmative words for the future? Same. You want it a lot, but it hasn't happened yet, so that doubt still has room to fester and grow into worry.

But what if you spoke your affirmation in the present tense?

What is the difference between saying "money comes into my life quickly" compared to "I have all the wealth I will ever need"?

In the first example, in future tense, you know the Universe will provide, but you don't have it yet, which means you are not grateful for having received it, and there is still the possibility that it may not materialize, and your financial stresses could become even worse and so on. There is still room for those doubts and worries to crowd into your brain.

But with the simple phrase, "I have all the wealth I will ever need," you can express your gratitude and can feel that happiness and success. You have what you need!

By imagining you already have it, there is no room for doubt; it's done, it's already happened. Your body begins to feel the excitement, gratitude, and joy that you would feel when it comes to pass, even though it hasn't actually, in the real world, come to pass, yet! But by expressing your gratitude and behaving as if you have already received the blessings, the Law of Attraction more often than not, if it is the right thing for you, brings it to you because your subconscious mind believes it exists already.

In *The Game of Life and How to Play It*, Florence Scovel Shinn provides many examples of interactions with others in which they expressed their fear, doubt, and feelings of lacking, and consequently brought lack and loss into their lives.

Visioning vs. Visualizing

*"Many a man is building for himself in imagination
a bungalow when he should be building a palace."*
—Florence Scovel Shinn, *The Game of Life and How to Play It*

Though the terms "vision" and "visualize" sound similar, and most dictionary definitions would assign them the same meaning, in the case of metaphysics and manifesting your desires, there is a distinct difference between the two.

Florence states that she was often asked the difference between visualizing and visioning, and her response was thus:

"Visualizing is a mental process governed by the reasoning or conscious mind; visioning is a spiritual process, governed by intuition, or the superconscious mind. The student should train his mind to receive these flashes of inspiration, and work out the 'divine pictures,' through definite leads. When a man can say, 'I desire only that which God desires for me,' his new set of blueprints is given him by the Master Architect, the God within.

God's plan for each man transcends the limitation of the reasoning mind and is always the square of life, containing health, wealth, love, and perfect self-expression. Many a man is building for himself in imagination a bungalow when he should be building a palace."

We all have specific goals that we dream of. We want a specific job, or a particular person to love us back, or to be rewarded after all of our hard work and training to stand on the championship podium. But these are goals of the conscious, reasoning mind, and that job, person, or sport may not be the right thing. It may not be in the Divine Plan for you in life.

It can feel contradictory but, instead of praying for and visualizing the specifics of your desires, marrying *that* person, being successful in *that* job, scoring the winning goal as a member of *that* favored team, you should make your affirmations less specific.

Think about it. You want a happy and successful future, but what if that desired lover, job, or team is not going to make you as happy as you think it will? You want love from the person who is destined for you; you want the career that you will thrive in, and to make it onto the team that allows you to excel, whatever person, job, or team it may be.

If you are happy, successful, and fulfilled in your life, you won't even care that it is not with that person, company, or team you thought it would be.

So using visioning in your affirmations, call the right opportunity to you, not the single one you desire, instead of visualizing. Your future will be better for it.

The Benefits of Vision Boards

Some people find it helps to create a vision board of their dream life so that they can have it in front of them constantly and remember to bring their focus back to the life they desire, even when life gets busy.

And life *does* get busy. It gets distracting with work or school, kids and cleaning, partners or dating, socializing, sports, and side hustles. The days can blur together and weeks pass as quickly as days. A lot of manifesting and the use of affirmations come in the form of thoughts or spoken word. Without something visibly sitting in front of you to remind you to take a moment—or several—every day to focus on and attract your dream life into being, it can be easy to forget to do it.

What Goes on a Vision Board?

Find images that represent your desires, whether this includes a well-furnished home, a thriving business, a wedding, a happy family, a winner's trophy, a tropical holiday, a college acceptance letter, or whatever it is you want for yourself.

Magazines, websites, or apps like Instagram and Pinterest are full of aspirational images you can save and print to stick to your board. Often people use corkboards and pins so that they can change up their vision board when their desires are fulfilled or they have new dreams. Another option is to tape your images directly to a wall, around a mirror, or inside a closet door if you want to keep it private.

Add one or multiple affirmations to your vision board and place it somewhere you will see it daily.

Remember, choose images that are representative of your wishes, not images of the specific dreams you have, such as a specific partner or acceptance to a specific college. This is a vision board, not a visualizing board, so the goal is to bring you what is right for you and in the Divine Plan for your life. It may not be the person or school you hoped for, but it will be the one that is right for your journey.

Don't Forget to Take Action!

It is one thing to manifest your desires toward you, thinking positively, and concentrating on health, prosperity, and love coming into your life. But once the Universe presents it to you, you must step in. God, or the Universe, has done its part; for example, if it brings the person into your life that you are going to find happiness with but you do not speak to them or you ignore their attention, there is only so much the Universe can do to help you along.

CHAPTER 8

The Power of Gratitude

Gratitude can change lives, and not only your own. In *The Power of the Spoken Word*, Florence is quoted as stating, "Man's part is to be a grateful receiver." But why is it so important to be grateful? Making a conscious decision to practice gratitude forces you to stop, be present in the moment, and reflect on your day, your year, or your life, which you may not have done before or in a long time. And when we stop to be grateful, the change in our own demeanor has a ripple effect out into the world, changing how we interact with those around us and how they interact with those around them.

Modern life is busy. We get so caught up with school runs and nightly routines, with project management and meetings, that we rush through our lives often without taking the time to stop and think about how it's going and how we feel. We're often in such a rush we push through every activity to get them over with and onto the next. We get so caught up in forward thinking about the destination that we don't live in the moment and appreciate the journey.

The jog you went on to burn off the extra calories from brunch also energized you and made your body feel good; the new art on the wall in the foyer at work is beautiful and calming; your colleague nailed their presentation at the team meeting, and you are proud of them and make a strong team together.

Stopping and taking the time to reflect and be grateful can make you realize that stressful days weren't as bad as you thought, difficult experiences in the past made you better prepared for others in the future, and there is beauty all around you if you make the effort to look around and appreciate it.

Making time to recognize things you're grateful for makes you happier, lowers stress levels, and even helps you get more restful sleep. Gratitude strengthens your resilience to adversity and emotional turmoil. Being thankful can make you more optimistic, compassionate, and forgiving.

But don't keep it all to yourself! Be generous with your gratitude. Acknowledging good deeds by others, showing that you have noticed that they are trying or doing well or were helpful, etc., can make you both feel good. Both the giver and the receiver of the pleasant surprise of your kind words or actions will benefit.

Expressing your gratitude to others, be they friends, family, colleagues, or even strangers who do you a kindness, brings joy to their day, strengthens bonds, and encourages them to continue practicing kindness, which could spread throughout your community as well.

Whatever it was that you were grateful to them for, whether it was big or small, it can never go wrong to tell them.

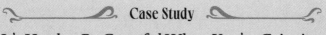 **Case Study**

It's Hard to Be Grateful When You're Grieving

Vince had a wonderful relationship with his mother, Olivia. They were the best of friends. Olivia raised Vince on her own as a single parent, and they had been through a lot. Their bond was unbreakable. But as she aged, Olivia started to become forgetful. She'd find the house keys in the fridge and wonder what they were doing there, and it would take her some time to remember that the child in front of her was her granddaughter. She was soon diagnosed with Alzheimer's disease.

Vince could not be grateful for this disease robbing him of his beloved mother. He felt angry and cheated as she was in good health otherwise. She potentially had years of life left with him as his lifelong best friend, the woman who would do anything for him, and he for her.

But there was nothing he could do to bring her memories back. To take away the polite smile on her face as he, a stranger, walked into her room, until she remembered or overlooked the fact that he was her beloved son.

Vince fell into a depression. He hid it from Olivia, as she didn't understand. How could he be grateful to God or the Universe for robbing him of his mother?

Vince didn't want to live his life angry and resentful. He felt the emotions taking a toll on his relationships with others. He was becoming irritable and short-tempered with his wife, and he felt a tightness in his chest. He was distracted at work, sleeping poorly, and as Olivia's memories retreated and hid from her, Vince turned further into himself, not wanting to share his pain.

But one day he knew he had to change. He didn't want to be this angry person anymore. He didn't want to treat his wife and daughter badly. He cherished his family and wanted to cultivate the loving upbringing he had with Olivia for his own daughter.

He was not ready to be grateful to Alzheimer's disease and its effect it had on his relationship with his mother, but he could be very grateful for the happy times he spent with her and all the happy memories they shared together. He could also be grateful that she wasn't in physical pain as her memories faded, that he still got to be with her. He was grateful for the legacy she left, the life lessons she taught him that he could pass on to his own daughter. The family traditions that he would continue after she was gone, to honor her and keep her memory alive within himself.

When he spent time with Olivia, instead of anger and grief and hurt at becoming a stranger to her, he told her their favorite stories, about trips they had been on and funny experiences they had shared. He read her favorite books and kept her room bright with her favorite flowers. They laughed together, and she enjoyed her time spent with this generous, compassionate man and his happy stories.

With gratitude, Vince chose acceptance.

He felt lighter. He enjoyed the time he spent with Olivia, even as her memories faded. With his new experience he was able to support a friend when her parent was similarly diagnosed and provide her comfort and a way forward.

And he found peace.

CHAPTER 9

The Divine Design

"There is for each man, perfect self-expression. There is a place which he is to fill and no one else can fill, something which he is to do which no one else can do; it is his destiny!"

—Florence Scovel Shinn,
The Game of Life and How to Play It

There is a reason you are on this planet, and though it is your job to find out what it is that you were made to do, don't force your conscious dreams onto your life's Divine Design. You may not have the faintest idea what that may be, and even if at some point you think you do, it is unfortunately common to experience a midlife or even quarter-life crisis in which you feel psychic and emotional pain, confusion, and doubt as to whether you are making a difference in the world—whether you are living the life you were meant for.

This can come about because you have resisted the Divine Plan for you and trusted your conscious mind instead, making your own plans, what your logical brain thinks is best, rather than letting go and allowing God or the Universe to guide you toward the life that will make you happy.

You may desperately desire to have a farm of your own, for example. A perfectly wonderful desire. But unbeknownst to you, you actually have a dormant, incredible talent in something you have never tried before that is your path to happiness, health, and prosperity more than farming would be. By forcing your focus and being specific with it, you may get exactly what you asked for, which would not bring the joy and success that you thought it would.

The Divine Plan of Your Life

"The Divine Plan of my life cannot be tampered with. It is incorruptible and indestructible. It awaits only my recognition."
—Florence Scovel Shinn, *Your Word Is Your Wand*

There is a Divine Plan for every person, and it is up to us to listen to God, the Universe, or whatever higher power we believe in, and find it.

As children we are often asked "What do you want to be when you grow up?" and as teenagers we are encouraged to choose a career path and select classes, apprenticeships, and college courses that will get us into that career, even when we have no lived experience of what the job or industry as a whole is like.

And why are we in charge of choosing, anyway?

As mentioned earlier, oftentimes, people spend a decade or more studying and then working in an industry, only to feel ready for a complete change. We develop skills and extensive years of experience over our time working but find ourselves unfulfilled. The job wasn't what we thought it would be when we were starry-eyed teenagers being asked to navigate the direction of our futures. It's a lot of responsibility to put on a teenager. You don't necessarily know what you're good at, yet. You don't even know all the different jobs and industries out there that you might enjoy or thrive in. You don't know what outside-the-box opportunities are out there via a possible different path.

In *The Game of Life and How to Play It*, Florence says, "I have known people to suddenly enter a new line of work, and be fully equipped, with little or no training."

I must agree with her. How many times have you seen adults in middle age or even their twilight years begin a new career and experience the most staggering success?

Stan Lee, creator of Marvel Comics, created his first comic, *The Fantastic Four*, at age thirty-nine.

Arianna Huffington launched the news juggernaut website *The Huffington Post* at fifty-five.

Sam Walton opened a little store you might know at age forty-four. That store is called Walmart.

Julia Child worked in advertising and media but wrote her first cookbook at age fifty, which set her on the path to become a renowned celebrity chef.

Harland "Colonel" Sanders franchised his chicken restaurant at age sixty. That restaurant is Kentucky Fried Chicken (KFC).

Each may have had perfectly fine careers over their lifetime, but once they followed their Divine Plan, found their place in the world, and embraced the thing they were best at, their lives changed in spectacular ways.

Case Study

Disappointing "Dream Jobs"

From early childhood, Hannah had dreams of being an editor in publishing. She dreamed of spending her days reading and being paid for it, rubbing shoulders with celebrity authors, and luxuriating in a world of creative thinkers bringing imaginary worlds to life.

She worked hard in high school, studied English and literature, and continued her studies after high school to complete her English degree. Overcoming fierce competition through the years, she accepted several roles in the industry, but it turned out the job she always dreamed of spending her life doing wasn't everything she had imagined. The hours were long, the pay was too low while the workload too high, and it took a lot of effort helping authors polish their sometimes ugly, uninteresting drafts into the magic that readers pick up from the bookshelves.

It was difficult for Hannah to accept that though she had achieved her dream, it left a lot to be desired and perhaps it was time to move on and find something else that did make her happy. But what would that be? It was supposed to be editing novels. It was always going to be editing!

After several years of continued stress and unhappiness in her career, she stopped resisting and made the scary move into the unknown: an unrelated industry where she could still utilize the skills she had honed over the decades of her life.

And suddenly, she was thriving as a project manager in local government. She discovered skills in project management that she didn't know she had simply because she had never needed to use them before. She was naturally tech-savvy and found it rewarding to be able to help others and her colleagues. Over the years she had developed natural leadership skills and in the new role had opportunities to utilize them. Though this career change had never been a part of her own plan, considering she was so unexpectedly successful and personally fulfilled in this new industry and the work she did, it was clearly part of the Universe's Divine Plan for her.

A Note on Florence Scovel Shinn and the Laws of the Universe

It must be acknowledged that some of the beliefs found in Florence's salons, lectures, and books from the early to midtwentieth century are outdated and a remnant of that time in history. Science has long since proved them inaccurate. For example, Florence decried the human carnal mind as the source of disease. They do not exist in the superconscious so, as a product of the human imagination, we can rid ourselves of disease through positive thinking and declarations that they do not exist.

Yes, a positive mindset and affirmations can certainly help the body fight off disease as it can help increase your resilience, but it is dangerous to rely solely on practicing manifestation of good health in order to feel well again.

Similarly, practicing positivity and cognitive behavioral therapies is very important for sufferers of chronic depression, anxiety, PTSD, or other mental illnesses, but forcing positive thinking alone won't necessarily adjust a chemical or hormonal imbalance that could be corrected through medical intervention, give sufferers relief, and help them feel mentally stronger and more able to focus on the good.

Ultimately, what I'm saying is that when you are unwell, seek medical attention when you need it and allow medicine to work in combination with any affirmations, prayer, or manifestation practices.

The Law of Attraction does not work by itself. You may successfully attract your desires, such as access to the right medicine, to you, but it is still up to you to take action and use it as the Divine Design cannot impress itself into your life without your acceptance and input.

CHAPTER 10

The Laws of the Universe

"The simple rules are fearless faith,
nonresistance, and love!"

—Florence Scovel Shinn,
The Game of Life and How to Play It

We're not talking about the scientific laws of the Universe here, but the laws regarding the unseen energies that affect how we think, feel, and live. Each law and the manner in which you work with or against it will impact your life and those around you.

Everything happens right when it's supposed to. For example, say you desperately want to be in a relationship. You are in your mid- to late-twenties, and many of your friends are coupling up and getting engaged. You're happy that they have found love, even as you look for your own partner. Your friends have less time for you as they embark on their married lives and begin to have and raise children. They begin to focus inward on their family unit (as you would expect them to), and as you hope to do when you find your perfect partner.

Growing into adulthood, this is a common scenario for one or two members of every friendship group, or among siblings: someone is going to be the last to fall in love, if they do at all.

But why has everyone around you found their love and started their life journeys together, while you haven't found yours?

Because, according to the laws of the Universe, everything happens right when it's supposed to. Have patience and trust that the world will bring you what is yours when you are ready for it.

Perhaps you are not as ready for a relationship as you think you are. Or you're not ready for the *right* relationship that will be everlasting and full of love. You may not be mature enough, or you may have some personal growth to do, some experiences that you need to undertake or lessons you need to learn in order to be ready and right for the person you're destined for. Or, they may need to learn before they meet you, so that you are on the same page, with the same goals and desires to move forward in unison and make a happy life together.

Growing up, many women are attracted to "bad boys." They like the thrill and excitement of being with someone who flouts the rules. But if your desire for your life is security, a stable home, and a family, a "bad boy" probably isn't going to make you happy and secure, or be a good role model for children. And that's fine for them, but it means they might not be right for you. They may have different and incompatible goals for their life, or they have growth to do before they shape into the type of man that will be a good, secure parent who can make you happy and become the type of partner you desire.

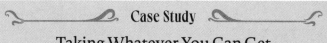

Case Study

Taking Whatever You Can Get

Ang has been having a tough time on the job market. He hasn't been able to secure a permanent full-time job in his dream career as he'd hoped to. To support himself he has settled for eclectic short-term jobs through recruitment agencies. Freelancing in this manner is not what he wants. It feels unstable and insecure, with potential unemployment at the end of every contract. He also feels like he isn't utilizing his skills, but heck, he needs an income so he's happy to accept whatever he can get.

Though he is grateful to be employed, he is somewhat disheartened. These unrelated roles don't lead him to feel like he is on his right path, even though he takes some time each day to speak his affirmations to attract his dream life to him.

After several short-term contracts in different industries and departments, however, Ang gains a breadth of experience and well-rounded expertise that make him a valuable candidate—the perfect candidate, even—for his dream job. With the experience he has gained he's confident that he could excel in his dream job or move into more highly paid positions.

While the short-term roles may not have felt right at the time, they enabled him to grow and learn and helped him build up the experience he needed in order to be the perfect candidate for the type of job he desired.

❁ The Law of Magnetism

"When you are fearful you begin to attract the thing you fear: you are magnetizing it."
—Florence Scovel Shinn, *The Power of the Spoken Word*

In scientific theory, the most basic law of magnetism is like polarities repel one another, and unlike polarities attract each other. Therefore, if you held two magnets together and directed either both positive poles or both negative poles toward each other, they would pull away. You would not be able to connect them. But if you faced a positive pole toward a negative pole, they would snap together, as the opposite poles attract each other.

This is not so in the Law of Magnetism in metaphysical theory.

When applying the concept of magnetism to people, saying something like, "Wow, he has such a magnetic personality" always means you find this aspect of them attractive. In metaphysical theory, magnetism refers to attracting your desires to you. It is always pushing the two magnets together, not pulling the two magnets apart.

However, you must be careful about what you focus on because doing so will bring more of that to you.

For example, Florence instructs not to say, "Poor Andrew" when he experiences a disappointment, as you will magnetize more misfortune to him. Instead, use your word as your magic wand and say, "lucky Andrew!" in order to help turn his fortunes around.

Try not to dwell on your fears as you will only bring them into reality.

―――――― ⌒ Case Study ⌒ ――――――

Expect the Worst, Experience the Worst

As a first-time home buyer, Jacob was stepping into a new arena, all on his own. On a single-income budget, he decided to build a brand-new house farther from the city rather than buy a fixer-upper closer to town because it could potentially cost him a lot more in repairs and renovations over time.

He thought he had done his homework before making any decisions. He tried to educate himself on everything that was involved and stick to his budget, but everything that could go wrong did.

Jacob found some land he liked and builders who agreed that the house could be built within the constraints of his tight budget. With the price settled, they told him to put down his deposit with the vendor to secure the land. He then returned to the builders to sign his construction contract. Only then did they announce there would be an additional site cost not included in the price they had originally provided him, to the tune of tens of thousands of dollars, and that the house design he had fallen in love with couldn't be built on his land, so he would need to start afresh.

Over budget, he would not be able to secure a loan to cover the additional costs, so he was now stuck with land he could not afford to build on.

Having purchased the land for the specific house plan at the specific promised price, he could not find another builder who could build his house for the price he could afford. He would need cheaper land in order to build to his budget.

But if he could not build on the land, he would lose his significant deposit and potentially receive a default on his credit score, meaning no bank would provide him a loan. He would not be eligible to build a house any time soon— even if he *could* still afford it. Every alternative plan he made, every option he investigated, turned out negatively and cost more and more money.

As his eye-opening first experience of building a house continued, he came to expect that every option would end in disaster and felt anxious and enraged at every conversation about trying to build his house. As he began to expect everything to go wrong, sure enough, it did. He attracted the worst-case scenario to him at every stage.

Finally, Jacob decided he'd had enough. He had reached a point in which he was waiting for the bank to approve his mortgage. He could have continued to worry as he waited; he could have allowed the stress and anxiety of not knowing if he would be approved to own his own home eat him alive. Instead, Jacob decided that he had no control over how long the bank was going to take, and his worry and stress and sleepless nights about it weren't going to make them approve it any faster.

Jacob decided to let go. To be nonresistant. What was going to happen was going to happen. He told himself that the loan was his. He had everything he needed, enough to build the house he desired.

And he was right. He became a magnet for good, for the process to become a smooth journey. From then on, each time a problem arose, Jacob told himself that everything was working out, the house was his. It was all going to plan. He remained clear-headed and calm instead of anxious and stressed. He believed everything was going to work out as he hoped. So it did.

He experienced a steep learning curve when it came to what was involved in building a house and how many additional costs and fees needed to be accounted for, but through the difficulties he learned a great deal and would certainly be more prepared and knowledgeable next time. And he moved into his brand-new home of his own.

✼ The Law of Attraction

"You attract the things you give a great deal of thought to."
—Florence Scovel Shinn, *The Secret Door to Success*

The Law of Attraction is the big kahuna in the modern metaphysical space. Next to the Law of Karma (page 82), it is the law of the Universe with the highest profile in modern society. The Law of Attraction is much talked about in the wellness industry, as well it should be.

Simply put, the Law of Attraction is the belief that you attract more of what you think about the most, be it positive or negative.

Manifestations (page 17), affirmations (page 40), visualization (page 46), and gratitude (page 51) can all invoke the Law of Attraction.

For example, Florence writes in *Your Word Is Your Wand*, "With love usually comes terrific fear. Nearly every woman comes into the world with a mythical woman in the back of her mind who is to rob her of her love."

Florence speaks of "the other woman," and whether she exists or not, insecure partners can manifest her into being by expecting that she exists. Florence says, "So long as she visualizes interference, it will come."

If you find yourself jealous when your partner spends time around others you think are attracted to them, then your focus on the prospect of your partner being unfaithful could very well cause them to be unfaithful. You can easily destroy a once-happy and committed relationship through suspicion, mistrust, and jealousy. Negative beliefs and emotions when thinking about your partner could hurt them emotionally. They may not want to be in a relationship with someone who doesn't trust them, who thinks that they would be unfaithful. Consequently, they could leave you and look elsewhere for a partner who does.

On the flip side, if you spend most of your time looking for the good in others, being helpful and generous and accepting there will be bad days but everything will work out in the end, then you attract others to treat you with the same helpful attitude and generosity of spirit as you offer them. By demonstrating generosity and love to others, in turn, you will attract it back to you.

In *The Game of Life and How to Play It*, Florence states that "stage-fright has hampered many a genius." We have all either experienced this undeniable truth about stage fright ourselves or witnessed someone else going through it, either to overcome it successfully or fail spectacularly and leave, humiliated and committed never to expose themselves to the experience again.

Whether on the stage or off, fear can prevent you from reaching out and grabbing your dreams with both hands. Instead, fear allows them to slip away.

A life lived in fear is a life that will end filled with regret. Act as if you are not afraid, and soon you won't be.

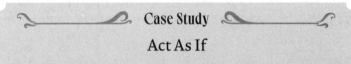

Case Study

Act As If

We've all heard the sayings "Act as if…" and "Fake it 'til you make it". These two phrases are important bedrocks in the Law of Attraction philosophy: you attract more of what you think about.

Imani is a good example of this philosophy in play. When reading the key selection criteria for a job Imani really wanted, she wasn't sure that she had all of the skills and experience that were required. But instead of limiting herself, rejecting herself from the job before the interviewers had the opportunity to, she decided to apply anyway. Who knew? Maybe she had other skills and experience that were just as valuable, or she could be one of the best candidates the employers would receive and they'd be happy to mentor and train her on what she didn't yet know.

Imani was thrilled when she received an interview, but again, not positive that she had all of the experience the job required. She was riddled with nerves.

In an effort to combat those nerves, Imani spoke affirmations of confidence, that she was successful and prosperous in the right role for her, and she had developed new skills that helped her thrive in the role. She focused her mind on this affirmation right up until her interview, and her nerves and insecurities began to subside as she focused on them less and less.

On the day of the interview, Imani acted as if.

Instead of allowing her nerves and insecurity to show and get the better of her, Imani straightened her posture, held her head high, and changed her behavior to that of a person who was confident in their abilities to perform well in the role. She acted as if she didn't lie at her interview or exaggerate her abilities, but exuded confidence and friendliness and did not allow her nerves to cloud her brain. And she got the job! She had more relevant skills and experience than she realized, and her new employers were happy to train her in what she was lacking.

Acting as if you are already successful, or faking it until you make it, forces your subconscious mind to believe you are successful and therefore pulls success toward you.

When the Glass Appears Half Full

Whether they are actively practicing it or not, the Law of Attraction is the key to many people's success and contentment in life. Those who look at the world optimistically, seeing the glass as half full, give others the benefit of the doubt, never assuming the worst in them. If they believe in the good of their community and aim to be helpful and make a positive impact, they are going to attract more good into their lives than bad. This optimistic attitude will attract others to them who share their values and, thus, shape their life.

But if you are pessimistic about the world, distrustful, expect the worst of others and believe that they will always try to swindle you—if you see yourself as a failure and resent the success of others, you are keeping away your own success and drawing this negativity and failure toward you.

In *The Secret Door to Success*, Florence says, "Your big opportunity and big success usually slide in, when you least expect it. You have to let go long enough for the great Law of Attraction to operate. You never saw a worried and anxious magnet. It stands up straight and hasn't a care in the world, because it knows needles can't help jumping to it."

It makes a lot of sense, if you think about it. Magnets only attract what they are created to: magnetic objects. They only pull what they are designed for toward them, so there is no need to worry and weaken that magnetic pull because everything will work out as it should.

Florence goes on: "I say in my correspondence course, 'Do not let your heart's desire become your heart's disease.' You are completely demagnetized when you desire something too intensely. You worry, fear, and agonize."

By allowing your conscious mind to worry about what will happen if you do not achieve your goals or your desire does not come to pass, you weaken its ability to attract. Your subconscious mind only understands what you believe and focus on, so if you focus on your lack, on your potential failure rather than on the joy of having what it is you desire, the subconscious mind will bring what you are focused on: lack and failure.

Be Careful What You Wish For

The Right Love, Not Just Any Love

In *The Game of Life and How to Play It*, Florence describes when she met with a woman who was completely, head over heels infatuated with a man, whom she called "A. B." Most of us can relate to this woman's experience of desperately wanting to be in a relationship with a particular person. She asked Florence to "speak the word," to cast affirmations into the Universe on her behalf, full of belief, power, and conviction, that she would marry him.

Florence refused. She explained to the infatuated woman that it would be a violation of spiritual law to ask the Lord or the Universe for this specific man to marry this woman. Instead, Florence said she would speak affirmations for the right man—the man who belonged with her by divine right. She added, "If A. B. is the right man, you can't lose him, and if he isn't for you then you will receive his equivalent."

The woman went away, and though she saw A. B. often, he appeared none the more romantically interested in her than he had before. The woman found her interest in him waning. Not long afterward, she met another man who fell in love with her immediately and treated her in exactly the ways that she had hoped A. B. would if they were together. She soon fell in love with him as well and had everything she wished.

The Law of Attraction provided a substitute and attracted the right man, for the Universe knew that A. B. was not the one for her. She suffered no loss or sacrifice in not marrying A. B., as she found the love and happiness she had craved from him elsewhere.

Had the woman persisted in visualizing her life with A. B., continued to pursue him, and forced the Universe to do her bidding rather than accepting that a higher power knew best, she may not have led a happy life with him. Or maybe she would have found a content life, but divergent from her path to success, prosperity, and the Divine Plan in store for her.

"Man sees first his failure or success, his joy or sorrow, before it swings into visibility from the scenes set in his own imagination. We have observed this in the mother picturing disease for her child, or a woman seeing success for her husband."

—Florence Scovel Shinn, The Game of Life and How to Play It

You Feeling Lucky?

If you think back and reflect on the positive and negative experiences, successes, and failures of your life thus far, I am sure you will remember times you felt unlucky and the Universe proved you right, or times you felt lucky or confident and the Universe provided for you. Do any examples come to mind? Many of us go through a funk when everything feels like it is going wrong, and it does. You may sail through it but hit every rough wave and think that's just how life is. You may come to the conclusion that you're just not very lucky.

A very successful woman in my own life once told me that she has always felt lucky, that things simply tend to work out. And they do. By thinking of herself as lucky, focusing her thoughts on thrilling experiences on the horizon, having the confidence that her dreams will come true, her subconscious knows only these positive outcomes ahead of her and manifests success, attracting it to her.

In my own life, when I was down on my luck, working an exhausting, underpaid, overworked job that I had desperately wished for (it was my dream job!), I used to worry about the future. I would fret and focus on the fear that I would not be able to support myself, that my dreams would always be fruitless no matter how hard I worked toward making them a success.

I just wasn't very lucky.

While I focused on worst-case scenarios and my fears of failure and poverty, I remained stuck there, too stressed about my lack and loss to strive for my dreams or trust in a Divine Plan for me. I had focused so hard on attaining this specific job, manifesting it into my life, and shoehorning myself into a career that was not the right position for me and was all the worse for it.

Then I opened my mind to alternative paths and followed a Definite Lead (as discussed on page 23) into a completely different industry, with less work for significantly more money. With that boosted income my future is looking more secure, the overwork and overwhelm have subsided, and I have the capacity to focus and strive for my dreams.

I have a different mindset now. Sure, I still get stressed, overwhelmed, anxious, and depressed, but deep in my soul I now believe that, no matter how hard things may be right now, they will turn out okay in the end. I feel lucky.

I wanted to write another book but wasn't sure of what the topic should be. Then, out of the blue, I was contacted with an offer to write this very book! If that's not the Law of Attraction in action, what is?

❋ The Law of Prosperity

> "If one asks for success and prepares for failure,
> he will get the situation he has prepared for."
>
> —Florence Scovel Shinn,
> *The Game of Life and How to Play It*

Everybody wants to be prosperous. It's not greed that inspires them, but the simple desire for financial stability, security, and ability to provide for their family and not fear the next bill that arrives or how to make ends meet each week.

When finances are tight, it can feel like the logical and responsible choice to rein in your spending, perhaps by skipping your daily latte from your favorite coffee shop and making instant at home instead. Or saying no to that outing your loved ones have invited you to.

What if an emergency happens? What if your child falls ill, or you have an accident and need to visit a doctor? What if you get a flat tire and need to buy a new one? If your bank account is empty, how are you supposed to pay a medical bill or fix your tire? How will you get to work? Could you lose your job? It's much more responsible to hoard whatever resources you still have when you're running out, just to be safe. Just in case.

The Law of Prosperity explains otherwise.

As you just learned in the Law of Attraction chapter, what you focus on is what you bring more of toward you. By worrying about your income, by dreading the next bill or mishap and fearing that moment you spend your last dollar, you are focusing on how little you have. The Universe doesn't care that you don't want it: you will receive more of what you focus on.

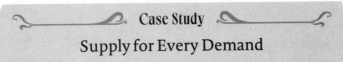

Case Study

Supply for Every Demand

In *The Game of Life and How to Play It*, Florence tells the story of a woman she counseled who was in desperate need of money, for she was surely about to be sued and had no way of finding the needed funds. Florence advised her that in God and the Universe, "there is a supply for every demand."

She advised that now was not the time to economize. She needed to act as if she already had the money, to go out to dinner like she was flush with riches. By acting as if she could easily afford it, the amount she owed would be completely within her means. She was to believe she had already received the money she needed and be grateful for her blessings.

The woman left Florence and called her a few days later, astounded at her change in fortune. The day came that she expected the bill and as hard as she focused and believed, she was none the richer. But then, a surprise visitor came to call: her uncle. As they caught up, she was loathe to admit her shame and despair, but as the visit wound up, he asked how her finances were.

She couldn't hold it in any longer; she confessed to her uncle that she was to be sued and had no money to pay it. To her shock, her uncle decided to write her a check for the amount that she needed.

Though the woman had no way of finding the money and could see no way it would come to her, she changed her focus from fear and lack to belief and gratitude for her prosperous life and attracted that prosperity to her precisely when she needed it.

❊ The Law of Karma

"Vengeance is mine, saith the Lord" (law)
Romans 12:19 as referenced in Florence Scovel
Shinn, *The Game of Life and How to Play It*

What Is Karma?

Karma is a Sanskrit word meaning "action." It is a philosophy predominantly found in Hinduism and Buddhism. Though the word is not often used in Western religious teachings, the concept is universal.

In the Christian Bible, karma is known as the concept of "reaping what you sow," which means that we are likely to receive the same blessings, or problems, we bestow on others.

Indeed, the Law of Karma is about cause and effect in the Universe. It teaches that whatever we put out into the Universe, we receive back. If we make decisions and act through greed, hurt, hatred, or fear, then we invite suffering into our own lives. But if our motivations are generosity, love, or wisdom, then we invite inner joy, peace, and prosperity into our lives.

> "Giving opens the way for receiving."
> —Florence Scovel Shinn,
> *The Game of Life and How to Play It*

You've likely heard people say "I'll let karma take care of them" or "Karma will get them." But what do they mean by that? If someone has wronged you, cheated you, or caused you pain, instead of holding onto anger and retaliating, you can rise above them and allow the Law of Karma and the Universe to deal out the consequences for their actions. You don't need to sully your soul and get even with those who wronged you. Keep your conscience clear. Karma will make sure they get what they deserve and nothing more.

When You've Been Wronged

It can be hard to let go of your hurt and anger, say, if your partner cheats on you, or perhaps a colleague uses your hard work to gain a business advantage for themselves. You'd feel heartbroken. Betrayed. You'd be furious, and justifiably so! They hurt you, made a fool of you, set you backward in your plans for your life. These feelings are perfectly valid; anyone would feel this way.

Allow yourself to feel the hurt. Experience it, then most importantly, let it go. Allowing that resentment and hatred to simmer inside and bury itself within you doesn't hurt the one who hurt you; the only person it continues to hurt is yourself.

> *"Man receives only that which he gives. [...]*
> *Man's thoughts, deeds and words, return to him*
> *sooner or later, with astounding accuracy."*
>
> —Florence Scovel Shinn,
> *The Game of Life and How to Play It*

You may want to even the score and inflict the pain that was inflicted upon you. If you decide to retaliate against those who wronged you, then you are only inviting that negativity, spreading it back to yourself. Will you really feel better after hurting someone else, even if they hurt you first? Chances are that you won't. You only hurt yourself further by acting in hateful ways and deliberately causing harm. You will have to live with those actions forever.

Instead, allow the Universe to provide those who do you dirty with repercussions for their wrongs. There is no need to tarnish your own soul. You may never know when karma will be enacted, or what those repercussions will be, but you can have faith that the Universe will take care of it for you.

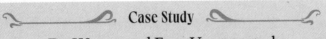

Case Study

Do Wrong and Face Unexpected Consequences

While on a family outing with his wife and two young children at the local aquarium, Simon took wonderful candid photographs of his children in the underwater tunnel. He wanted to capture the first time they saw a shark or a giant ray float peacefully above their heads. Using the camera on his cell phone would have been fine, but he had decided to bring his expensive, high-end camera that day, to take the best quality photos he could.

Simon and his family had a blast at the aquarium. He took some amazing photos, and the kids loved the aquatic creatures they saw.

In the gift shop on their way out, his children begged for some souvenirs and, though the day had been expensive, Simon didn't want to disappoint his children, or look stingy to his wife, so he let the children pick out some toys.

While ringing up their purchases, the cashier was momentarily distracted by a question from another customer. When the cashier returned their attention to Simon's purchases, Simon noticed that they had forgotten to scan one of the items. But he didn't say anything.

Simon and his family left the aquarium with all of their gift shop items, including a big, expensive stuffed toy shark they had not in fact paid for.

Simon was conflicted on the trip home. He knew he had done the wrong thing by not speaking up when the cashier missed scanning the shark. By not saying anything, the family had stolen the toy.

That evening, after the children were tucked into bed, Simon and his wife decided to look through the photos taken on the expensive camera. But where was it? They hunted through the bags they had taken with them and checked the car in case it had fallen out. But the camera—more expensive than the toy shark—was gone.

The loss of the camera was clear karmic punishment for Simon's theft of the toy shark. The aquarium staff didn't need to punish him, the Universe took control of the situation instead.

Good Karma

Karma isn't only vengeful, bringing about negative consequences to those who commit wrong. On the flip side, karma can also reward those who produce positive outcomes for other people, animals, their community, or even the planet. If you do not have ulterior motives or strings attached to your kind actions, and you act purely out of the goodness of your heart, then good karma will reward you.

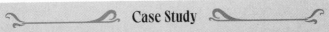

Case Study

Create Good for Others and Be Rewarded

Dan is a CEO of a Seattle business with 120 employees. He decided to take a significant pay cut in order to raise his employees' wages to a reasonable living wage of $70,000 per year. He reduces his pay to $70,000 a year as well. Dan wants his employees to be happy, to be able to support themselves and their families, and to live good lives. His lifestyle doesn't require the substantial salary of a tech company CEO, and he knows the money would make a fundamental difference to the lives of his employees.

He wants to take care of his employees out of the goodness of his heart, putting them ahead of profits.

And Dan is rewarded for it.

After his workforce receives a significant pay raise, they are less stressed, and happier at home and at work. Retention at the company increases as his staff feels valued and appreciated, which reduces the cost of hiring and training new employees.

With the staff being happier at work and feeling valued, productivity increases and, thus, revenue increases, with profit growth outpacing wage growth.

His employees start buying houses and the number of employees starting families rises significantly because they have that newfound financial security to get off the treadmill, stop living paycheck to paycheck, and start living.

Through word of mouth from ecstatic employees, Dan's generosity gains worldwide media coverage, not only attracting new customers who want to support a company that values their employees but inspiring other CEOs around the globe to follow his lead and provide better wages and conditions for their own employees.

After providing for his employees out of the goodness of his heart, Dan's business is thriving, and he is rewarded not only monetarily but through the pride and enjoyment of seeing his staff create the lives they always dreamed of.

Even if business hadn't also picked up, how amazing would it feel to be Dan, to have made that much of a difference in the lives of so many people he cares about, not because he needed to, but simply because he could?

> "In order to create activity in finances, one should give."
> —Florence Scovel Shinn, *The Game of Life and How to Play It*

In *The Game of Life*, Florence states: "Tithing, or giving one-tenth of one's income is an old Jewish custom and is sure to bring increase." Tithing is a worthy investment for both the giver and the receiver.

If you worry about money and paying your bills, focusing on how little you have and holding onto every cent, your subconscious and the Universe will conspire to give you more of what you are focused on: lack. It will not provide abundance and prosperity, which you so desperately desire but are not focused on.

As Dan in the previous case study found, when generous with your spirit and your wealth, not only does the receiver enjoy your unexpected bounty, but also you benefit as well. Dan's monetary gift multiplied and was returned to him by God, or the Universe, thus transforming him into a receiver himself.

If you repeat and demonstrate generosity of spirit, the subconscious brings generosity and abundance back to you.

❋ The Law of Forgiveness

Just as the Law of Karma ensures that those who wrong you will be punished accordingly, the Law of Forgiveness protects your soul and heart. Indeed, the Law of Forgiveness, or Grace, is stronger. It is a higher law that transcends that of karma. In the Christian faith you can find the Law of Forgiveness in *The Lord's Prayer*: "Forgive us our trespasses as we forgive those that trespass against us."

As long as you hold onto anger, judgement, and intolerance, letting them fester inside you, you won't find happiness. Whether someone betrayed you or even God, the Universe, or Mother Nature destroyed your home in a fire, flood, or tornado, if you hold onto the pain and resentment of your situation you will not be able to heal and move forward.

Karma looks out for you by taking action for you, leaving your soul unsoiled by the hunt for justice. Forgiveness allows you to move on, to keep from dwelling in sorrow or betrayal or hatred. It allows you to heal from the trauma, however big or small, and go forward with your life in peace. To deny forgiveness is to make yourself suffer. In turn, forgiveness from others for your own misdeeds allows you to move forward in peace.

Forgiveness doesn't mean you need to keep the person who wronged you in your life. It doesn't mean that you will allow everything to be the same as it was and give them opportunities to hurt you again. Forgiveness means you let go of the burden of those memories and trauma. You can walk away from those who caused you pain.

The Law of Forgiveness, as Florence explains in *The Game of Life and How to Play It*, also speaks of taking the power of forgiveness out of mortal hands, recognizing that it is for God or the Universe to forgive, even to forgive you.

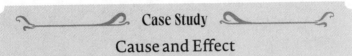

Case Study

Cause and Effect

In *The Game of Life and How to Play It*, Florence recounts a conversation she had with a distressed woman who didn't know what to do after she had received a counterfeit twenty-dollar note from the bank. She couldn't go back to the bank; they would never believe her, and she would be forced to leave, shamefaced and still without the much-needed money.

Florence ruminated with the woman and suggested they analyze why she had attracted the counterfeit cash to her. The woman knew at once; she had gifted a friend some stage money as a joke. Florence explained that the Law of Karma, which knew nothing about jokes, had given her back the stage money she had gifted.

Florence stated that they would call on the Law of Forgiveness in order to neutralize the situation.

"Infinite spirit," Florence said, "we call on the Law of Forgiveness and give thanks that she is under grace and not the law, and cannot lose this twenty dollars which is hers by divine right."

The woman returned to the bank, and to her pleasant surprise, the teller apologized courteously and exchanged the counterfeit note for a real one without fuss.

The Law of Forgiveness neutralized the Law of Karma that was enacted on the woman over a playful prank. It restored balance.

✽ The Law of Nonresistance

Let's be real, as hard as you may work to have a grateful heart and attract prosperity in every way you desire it, sometimes life simply sucks. No one gets through life without hitting rough seas. Bad things happen:

✤ Your house burns down.

✤ Your position at work is made redundant, or your business can't survive a lethal, worldwide pandemic, and you're left with nothing.

✤ A loved one dies.

✤ Or, worse still, hundreds, thousands, or millions of people die in a global catastrophe.

It's hard to be grateful for these things, right? And even if you have been saying your affirmations and words of gratitude for all that is coming to you as loudly as you can, envisioning your dream life in your mind's eye and making it so vivid you can almost feel, smell, and taste it. . . shit still happens.

It's awful, but according to the Law of Nonresistance, even these things happen for a reason.

Don't resist the lessons that God, or the Universe, is trying to teach you. Many people experienced heartbreak and lost their livelihoods, homes, or loved ones during the COVID-19 pandemic. Some had to move back in with family to save money they no longer had coming in. Others had to wait out lockdown to see if they might still have a job at the end of it, or find something new to support themselves. Still others had to forge ahead and create a new life without their partner, parent, or child. Absolutely devastating situations!

But for some, living under the same roof with their parents, grandparents, or their siblings again as the world slowed down was quality time they cherished and would not have had otherwise in the busyness of pre-pandemic life.

Some full-time-working parents got to take a breather and spend more quality time with their children than they ever had as they worked from home while their kids took part in distance learning. Others spent time video-chatting with loved ones as far away as across the globe or as close as the apartment next door when they never would have paused long enough to do so before. In some situations, it was lucky they did, as it was for the last time.

The pandemic's impact on businesses forcefully thrust many of those who had settled for an unfulfilling life or toxic workplace culture to get out of their comfort zone. They lost jobs they hated and got creative with how to earn an income. This showed them how many skills they didn't realize they had and how resilient and resourceful they could be.

When the world stood still, this allowed many people the time to work on that business idea they'd had for ages but couldn't find the time to develop— because of other commitments, such as work and school, family and friends.

For example, an Australian woman lost her retail job due to COVID-19 lockdowns. She brought a new hair product to market and blew up on TikTok. Making short videos in her home office-cum-warehouse, she turned her pandemic business into a million-dollar work-from-home empire.

Then there were the unhappy couples who were trapped together under lockdown, forced to confront the reality that their relationship wasn't working and needed to end. Many relationships ended due to lockdowns, but these individuals moved on, free to find the partner or life that was actually going to make them happy—perhaps with a new person, a new city or country, and a brand-new start at life.

And what about the two friends who started a business making Greek desserts from scratch and within a year sold it in a lucrative deal with a nationwide supermarket chain.

Live the Law of Nonresistance. Don't resist the bad experiences, as they might be teaching you something, opening your eyes to what you're capable of, making you emotionally stronger, or forcing you onto a different path—the right path. The Divine Path. The hardship you suffered will certainly help you be all the more grateful when the good comes.

Case Study

From Tragedy Came Prosperity

During the off-peak season in the holiday town they live in, my parents' home was surrounded almost entirely by empty vacation homes.

They went out with their dogs for the day, unaware that after enjoying toast for breakfast, the toaster lever had gotten stuck in the down position, so the toaster was unable to pop back up and switch off. The toaster grew hotter and hotter. While they enjoyed their day without a care in the world, their kitchen was catching on fire with no one around to see.

That same morning, a woman was enjoying her last morning on vacation in the town before packing her family up and returning to their regular lives. She decided to go for one final walk around the neighborhood before settling in for the long drive home. Something pushed her to walk an extra block than she had on other mornings—some intuition that made her keep walking.

On the next block, where all but one house was shut up and empty of life for the season, she heard a smoke alarm beeping.

As she reached my parents' house, smoke billowed from the windows. There was an explosion, and the kitchen window blew out. She dialed the fire brigade with one hand and grabbed the garden hose from the front yard with the other. Getting as close to the burning house as she dared, she aimed water through the broken window until the fire truck arrived.

There was no one else on the street. She hadn't planned to walk this way—hadn't planned on this final stroll around the neighborhood before packing up and going home. But by some divine timing she was exactly where she needed to be to stop the house from burning to the ground and potentially taking the vacation homes along either side with it. No one else would have seen it happening. My parents weren't going to be back for hours.

Yes, their kitchen was totally destroyed, the skylight had melted into a puddle of plastic on the floor, the electronics in nearby rooms had melted, and so much smoke had gotten through most of the house that without touching anything inside, you would exit the house covered in soot. But the house was still standing.

I'm not discounting the horrific reality of the house partially burning down, but it could have been far worse. It was still a traumatic experience for the woman on her stroll who saved their house, not knowing at the time whether people were inside and in danger.

When my father called the insurance company, he was relieved to hear some happy news: somehow, they had been overinsured for their house. Not only was the damage to the house covered and a new kitchen built (with changes and upgrades where necessary), but their belongings were taken away for cleaning and restoration, and they were given a generous budget at a big chain department store to replace what they wanted.

They were provided free accommodation in one of the empty vacation houses two doors down from their home until the new kitchen and repairs were complete. They lost some treasured belongings, including some family photo albums and personal artwork, but they did not lose the lives of any of the people in those photos or any belongings that they couldn't live without.

All was right because the woman on her vacation had been nonresistant to the sudden urge to walk that little bit farther.

CHAPTER 11

The Power of Your Spoken Word

> "We find in folk-lore and fairy stories,
> which come down from legends
> founded on Truth, the same idea—a
> word opens a door or cleaves a rock."
>
> —FLORENCE SCOVEL SHINN,
> *The Secret Door to Success*

In the Middle Eastern folktale *Arabian Nights* and Disney's *Aladdin* from the 1990s, the character Ali Baba faces the mountain and says "Open Sesame!" and the rocks slide apart. His barriers fall away, thanks to his spoken word.

What barriers might part in front of you when you voice the right words?

Have you ever been spoken to in a nasty way? Did your face heat up and your body recoil, filled with shame, humiliation, or perhaps, even fury? Your muscles may have stiffened, your eyes welled with tears, or your hands balled into fists. Your body may have screamed at you to flee, or maybe throw a punch.

Think about it. Due to someone else's words, you have almost certainly felt powerful emotions that may have impacted the way you see yourself or interact, especially if the words were said during your formative, youthful years.

Words are powerful. Everyone's words are. And it's your choice how you use them. Would you prefer to lift up, inspire, and encourage those around you, or push them down, belittle, and destroy? The choice, and the power you choose to wield, is yours.

Hype Beast

In *The Game of Life and How to Play It*, Florence compared words to winding up a Victrola. "We must wind ourselves up with spoken words" (page 39).

In other words, use your words to be your own hype man! Wind yourself up, be your very own personal trainer, be your football coach before the game. Rev your team of one up, get excited, talk animatedly either in your head or aloud, bounce on the balls of your feet, feel the urgency, get excited, get your adrenaline coursing, and envision and feel what it's going to be like to put that other team in the dirt and win.

Talk yourself into positive action. Feel the joy or peace or success of achieving your desires as you speak them into reality.

Your words have the power to change your life.

Hurt People Hurt People

Oftentimes, people hurt others because they are emotionally hurt themselves, and in order to get rid of the negative emotions inside, they lash out, ridicule, or upset someone else. But it doesn't make them feel better. It simply adds guilt to the hurt and potentially harms their relationship with the person they attacked.

For example, have you ever left a frustrating day of work feeling angry at your boss, then arrived home to find the house a mess or the dinner not started, then taken out your anger at your boss on your partner?

Imagine being in physical pain—either acute or chronic pain that wears you down over time. Someone touches your injury or bumps you when you're feeling sore all over, and you easily get angry at them for hurting you. But they didn't hurt you; you were already in pain.

Hurt people can overreact. It takes time to heal hurt—be it emotional or physical—but you can do so. If it is not yourself who is hurt, but a loved one, or even an acquaintance, practice the Law of Forgiveness and understand where they are coming from. Use the Power of Your Spoken Word and offer them kindness, showing that you care.

Pay Attention to How You Speak

Pay attention to what comes out of your mouth, especially when you're distracted or not thinking about it. Do you acknowledge your friend's pretty hairstyle or her ugly top? The things we say, especially when they're off the cuff and we're not choosing our words carefully, often betray our subconscious thought patterns.

By changing what you focus on and changing what you say, you can change how you think, and ultimately, change your circumstances for the better. Be your own best cheerleader! Not your worst bully.

CHAPTER 12

Modern-Day Additions to the Laws of the Universe

Since the 1940s, when Florence Scovel Shinn was at the peak of her influence, the concepts of New Thought and metaphysical theory that she taught have remained vastly the same. However, in the over eighty years that have passed since her time, more modern-day thought leaders have contributed additional laws to help you more acutely manifest your desires.

The following additional Laws of the Universe were not discussed in Florence's works but are certainly worthy of considering in your spiritual practice.

❋ The Law of Unwavering Desire

Sometimes you practice manifestation, speak affirmations, visualize and feel, yet the Universe does not appear to be listening. It can be easy for your faith to get a bit shaky and for doubts to set in. The Law of Unwavering Desire refers to these times, when you're trying your best to manifest something into your life but nothing appears to be working.

Take some time to reflect on your desires. Is what you're attempting to attract what you truly want? Maybe, over time, your conscious mind has infiltrated your affirmations and begun dreaming of a specific life for you that wasn't your original intention, or your desires have changed over time and no longer align with what you are still attempting to manifest.

You may be attempting to attract a million dollars into your life—or a billion! But is that what you truly, deep-down desire? Perhaps what you truly desire is simpler. Maybe at the core of it, you desire financial freedom—to have enough wealth that you don't need to look at the price on the menu and can be perfectly comfortable paying for the entire table without a care. Though you're trying to manifest an eight-figure income, perhaps you actually believe the more money, the more problems.

Perhaps you simply desire enough to be able to take time off from work and share new experiences with your family, such as trips abroad. You don't actually want a billion dollars;

you want financial freedom, whatever number that may turn out to be.

Maybe what you're asking of the Universe in terms of love isn't what you want anymore either. What if you once dreamed of a romantic partner who would sweep you off your feet with grand gestures like filling your house with red roses—someone who would shower you with gifts and whisk you away for luxurious vacations and to exclusive formal events. But over the years, you've mellowed, and grand gestures now look cringe-inducing— a waste of money that could be better spent. All those rose petals would need to be cleaned up afterward, you don't actually feel comfortable at fancy formal events, and you can't just drop everything and go on vacation—you have other important life commitments. Perhaps these days love looks like a few close friends and drinks around a bonfire. Or private time with your love's undivided attention.

Reflect on your desires and realign your affirmations with your true intentions. Be sure that you are crystal clear, that your dreams are so strong and unwavering that you convince your subconscious and the Law of Attraction can't help but bring them to you.

❋ The Law of Delicate Balance

Balance is a fundamental theme in the Law of Attraction. If our emotions are unbalanced then we can succumb to fear, anxiety, stress, and desperation. The conscious, logical brain can take over and we forget to express gratitude as our faith in the gifts of the Universe dwindles.

We need to reflect on our blessings and demonstrate gratitude and appreciation for what we already have. Only in this state of gratitude for the efforts and Divine Plan in place by a higher power will we receive and achieve more in the future.

By expressing gratitude, we can shun the negative energies and emotions of anxiety or fear, desperation, or obsession and return to a mental state of peace and balance, a place in which you will be ready to manifest your dreams and accept what the Universe has in store for you.

❋ The Law of Harmony

Similar to the Law of Delicate Balance, the Law of Harmony relies on our energy, thoughts, and emotions to be balanced. Sometimes our thoughts and values are disharmonious with our actions. They are not aligned. "Do what I say, not what I do," we might tell others. We don't practice what we preach.

When you are in a state of harmony within, you have a balanced mindset, one that is not full of fear or overcome with an obsessive desire for your dreams to come true. When you are in a state of harmony, you will find yourself more attuned with the Universe, the ability to tap into the energy around you, and higher powers.

The Laws of the Universe all lead to inner harmony. Being in a state of harmony is a culmination of many of the laws already discussed. You will be nonresistant, loving, forgiving, generous, and peaceful. The purpose of the Law of Karma is to achieve balance, and the purpose of the Law of Balance is to achieve a state of harmony. In this state, according to the Law of Harmony, you will be better connected, and your internal powers for manifestation heightened, bringing you greater abundance of your desires.

Your affirmations and manifestation practices will become all the more powerful when you are in harmony with the Universe, and abundance will be attracted toward you.

❄ The Law of Right Action

The Law of Right Action refers not to your thoughts or emotions, but the actions you choose to take in the world. This includes how you treat others, and the compassion and empathy you show to those around you. Basically, make good choices, okay?

What would you do if you found a purse on the ground at the bus stop? Looking inside, you find the ID of an elderly woman, and wads of cash. You could take the money; you have expenses this would help with as well, or luxuries you could never justify purchasing with your own hard-earned cash. And the Law of Attraction is about attracting prosperity to you, in sometimes unexpected ways, right?

But would taking this money from a senior citizen be the right thing to do? Would the Law of Attraction truly remove her wealth and hand it directly to you? How would it feel in your soul to have taken from someone in their twilight years? Doesn't sound like it would really gel with good karma, does it?

Even if the wallet did not belong to an elderly person, but a teenager, or a man in his forties. The owner of this money could be well off and the loss just an inconvenience, or it could be the last dollars they have to their name.

Returning the purse or wallet, including identification, cards, and cash, can only attract good to you. By returning the wallet, you may be saving the owner from some hassle and inconvenience, or you might be saving them from an eviction notice. You don't know.

Sure, you could take the money. But would it be the right action? And how would it make you feel when you spent it? If you have done so in the past, how did it make you feel? If you've found a wallet and handed it in to a police station or even delivered it to the house listed on the ID, how did you feel then? Spending the stranger's money compared to returning the lost belongings to their owner will evoke two very different emotions inside you, and you will receive two very different karmic consequences from the Universe.

As you make choices every day throughout your life, hold yourself to high standards. Choose the empathetic path, the way of dignity and compassion. Take the right actions that will allow you to hold your head up high. Just be a good human and enjoy the prosperous life you seek.

The Law of Universal Influence

According to the Law of Universal Influence, everything and everyone in the universe is connected. You being on this planet, being who you are, makes a difference to the world. I want you to take that in. You, being who you are, make a difference. You matter.

Since we are connected to the Universe, our thoughts, beliefs and even actions affect other people, even perfect strangers. Celebrities, influencers, politicians, academics, and even opinionated strangers on the internet or Letter to the Editor columns impact our lives, beliefs, desires, and how we see the world. And those who influenced their views and actions therefore affect you, too.

Think about someone whose thoughts and opinions you value. Their thoughts and opinions did not occur to them in a void. They were shaped by the influence of others— sometimes many others—as well as their upbringing and their life experience. Through their personal reflection and decision-making process they come to their own conclusions and take action.

You observe their actions and listen to their opinions, which may influence your own thoughts, desires, and actions. Then you express your thoughts and opinions and take action, which will influence others, and on and on it goes. Your personal influence is much more far-reaching than you realize.

If you follow the laws of the Universe and focus your energies on positivity and the good around you, rather than judging others, you can lead by example and inspire others to live happier, more empathetic, and more peaceful lives, too.

Everyone and everything is connected, so energy has the power to expand into every crevice of the world. As a tsunami fades to a wave, then to a ripple the farther it travels from the disturbance that caused it, so too does our own energy diminish as it leaves us. But like the tsunami creates devastation to everything in its path, your energy causes reactions in your environment as well.

When you scream with joy or yell in anger, those in the next room or even out in the street may get a shock, but those in the next town over will not hear you. The shock of the sudden scream can startle the person outside, unaware that it is a happy sound. Depending on their own life experience, they might rush in to help you, run away in fear, deciding it's an unsafe neighborhood and never return, or call the police and escalate a situation that never warranted it.

Your influence is a responsibility to take seriously. What influence do you want to have on the world?

Conclusion

The laws of the Universe and the religious teachings described within these pages are designed to help those who practice them build their self-esteem, change their mindset, and create a happier, healthier, more successful and peaceful life that they enjoy. The laws lay the foundation for improving the way you think, and therefore, how you feel and the actions you take, which can flow on and create change around you.

Practicing affirmations and looking for the good in the world rather than expecting or focusing on the worst can only help pull you out of depression and darkness. It can help you move through life with peace. As silly as it can feel to speak affirmations to God or the Universe, or whatever you believe is guiding you, the more often you practice it, the more natural it will feel and the more joy you will attract into your life.

Summary

- Know what you truly want.
- Focus on gratitude, empathy, and love.
- Be intentional with your communication.
- Visualize your success.
- Be accountable to yourself and others, and be open to change.
- Practice forgiveness and trust that God or the Universe will correct wrongs or imbalances for you.

.

CHAPTER 13

Affirmations

Life-Changing Affirmations by Florence Scovel Shinn

In this chapter, you will find affirmations for love, wisdom, success, prosperity, health, and a multitude of desires.

Some affirmations speak to God, others speak to the Universe, and still others don't mention either at all. If speaking to God doesn't feel comfortable to you or align with your beliefs, you can easily rephrase the affirmation to wording that feels right.

Similarly, if the sentiment in an affirmation addressing the Universe speaks to you but you'd prefer to be praying to God, rephrase and address God, or the higher power you have faith in.

Take as much or as little from the affirmations found here as you want, and tweak them to suit your goals as you will. Or, come up with your own!

Tips for Writing Affirmations

When writing your own affirmations, remember:

1. Use present tense. State that you already have your desires, not that you want them to come. And believe it!

2. Do not be too specific. Ask the Universe to bring you what is rightly yours and right for you (what you specifically want might not be it).

When speaking your affirmations and manifesting your desires, here are some tips to set you on the right path:

1. Take some time to yourself. You don't need to be alone, but you do not want to be disturbed. Take as long or short a time as you want.

2. Speak your affirmations anywhere you have a few minutes to be present. This can be while meditating, walking, driving, in bed, in the bath, or even while waiting somewhere.

3. Concentrate. See in your mind's eye and feel what it would be like if this desire were already yours. Hold that feeling for as long as you can, remember it, and bring it back often.

4. You can speak your affirmations aloud. "Your word is your wand," as Florence says. If you're not comfortable saying it aloud, you could chant your affirmation quietly in your head, write it down, or do whatever works for you.

5. If your mind is prone to wandering, writing affirmations down repeatedly can help you concentrate. Allocate a notebook for your private affirmation practice and fill the pages with them.

6. Repeat the affirmation again and again.

7. Be open to receiving well beyond your wildest dreams. Don't limit yourself.

8. Remember to breathe!

Pleasant Manifestation Experiences

You can speak your affirmations anywhere, such as in the car, while riding public transportation, or even on the sidelines at a sporting match. But some experiences are simply more peaceful, more enjoyable, and more in tune with your higher power than others.

Some relaxing and enjoyable ways to perform your affirmation and manifestation practice include:

1. Speaking your affirmations while walking. This can create a good rhythm as your words fall into pace with your steps.

2. Meditating. Breathing deeply, concentrating on your affirmations, and visualizing can create a tranquil manifestation experience.

3. Lighting a candle and gazing into the flame.

4. Taking a relaxing bath or warm shower in a misty bathroom with essential oils.

5. Sitting quietly in nature.

6. Lying in bed in the morning, before rising, while the world is still quiet. This can be a great way to start the day with the right intentions and your desires at the front of your mind.

Now that you have an idea of how you might want to practice your affirmations, sit quietly for a moment and think about what it is you hope to manifest into your life. Once you have a topic of particular interest, be it love, health, or prosperity, browse through the affirmations in the following pages and find what speaks to you

For Wisdom

Faith without nerve is dead. I have fearless nerve.

I never look, or I will never leap. I leap into
the unknown toward my desires.

God works in unexpected places, through unexpected
people, at unexpected times, and I don't question it.

Loving my neighbor means I do not limit my
neighbor in word, thought, or deed.

I never argue with a hunch.

The Kingdom of Heaven is the realm of perfect ideas.

It is dark before the dawn but the dawn
never fails. I trust in the dawn.

I never do today what my intuition says to do tomorrow.

I never hinder another's hunch.

Selfishness binds and blocks. My every loving and
unselfish thought has in it the germ of success.

I never tire of make-believing. When I least
expect it, I shall reap my rewards.

My faith is elastic. I stretch it to the end of my demonstration.

Before I call I am answered, for the Universe's supply precedes the demand.

What I do for others I am doing for myself.

Every act I commit while angry or resentful brings unhappy reaction. I act with compassion and love.

Sorrow and disappointment follow in the wake of deceit and subterfuge. The way of the transgressor is hard. "No good thing is withheld from him who walks uprightly."

There is no power in evil. It is nothing; therefore, it can only come to nothing.

Fear and impatience demagnetize me. Poise magnetizes. I am composed and magnetic.

Sure-ism is stronger than Optimism. I am sure.

Divine ideas never conflict. And the Universe's ideas for me are Divine.

I follow my hunches. The Infinite Spirit is never too late. Everything happens when it is designed to.

For Love

As I am one with God, the Undivided One, I am one
with my undivided love and undivided happiness.

The Light of the Christ within me now wipes out all fear, doubt,
anger, and resentment. God's love pours through me, an irresistible
magnetic current. I see only perfection and draw to me my own.

Divine Love, through me, now dissolves all seeming
obstacles and makes clear, easy, and successful my way.

I love everyone, and everyone loves me. My apparent enemy
becomes my friend, a golden link in the chain of my good.

I am at peace with myself and with the whole world. I love everyone,
and everyone loves me. The floodgates of my good now open.

For Success

The decks are now cleared for Divine Action, and my
own comes to me under grace in a magical way.

My seeming impossible good now comes to
pass, the unexpected now happens!

Endless good now comes to me in endless ways.

I give thanks for my whirlwind success. I sweep all before me for
I work with the Spirit and follow the Divine Plan of my life.

I am more than equal to this situation.

I am awake to my good and gather in the
harvest of endless opportunities.

Divine Order is now established in my mind, body, and
affairs. I see clearly and act quickly and my greatest
expectations come to pass in a miraculous way.

There is no competition on the spiritual plane. What
is rightfully mine is given me under grace.

The tide of Destiny has turned, and everything comes my way.

I banish the past and now live in the wonderful now,
where happy surprises come to me each day.

There are no lost opportunities in Divine Mind;
as one door shuts another door is opened.

The genius within me is now released. I now fulfill my destiny.

I make friends with obstacles and every one becomes
a stepping-stone. Everything in the Universe, visible
and invisible, is working to bring to me my own.

I give thanks that the walls of Jericho fall down and
all lack, limitation, and failure are wiped out of my
consciousness in the name of Jesus Christ.

I am now on the royal road of Success, Happiness, and Abundance; all the traffic flows toward me.

I will not weary of well-doing, for when I least expect it I shall reap.

There are no obstacles in Divine Mind, therefore, there is nothing to obstruct my good.

Rhythm, harmony, and balance are now established in my mind, body, and affairs.

New fields of Divine activity now open for me, and these fields are ripe with harvest.

Man's will is powerless to interfere with God's will. God's will is now done in my mind, body, and affairs.

God's plan for me is permanent and cannot be budged. I am true to my heavenly vision.

The Divine Plan of my life now takes shape in definite, concrete experiences leading to my heart's desire.

I do not resist this situation. I put it in the hands of Infinite Love and Wisdom. Let the Divine idea now come to pass.

My good now flows to me in a steady, unbroken, ever-increasing stream of success, happiness, and abundance.

I am in perfect harmony with the working of the law. I stand aside and let Infinite Intelligence make my way easy and successful.

I walk on holy ground. The ground I am on is successful ground.

New fields of Divine Activity now open for me. Unexpected doors fly open, unexpected channels are free.

What God has done for others He can do for me and more!

I am as necessary to God as He is to me, for I am the channel to bring His plan to pass.

I do not limit God by seeing limitation in myself. With God and myself all things are possible.

Giving precedes receiving and my gifts to others precede God's gifts to me.

Every man is a golden link in the chain of my good.

God cannot fail, so I cannot fail. "The warrior within me" has already won.

Thy Kingdom come in me, Thy will be done in me and my affairs.

For Prosperity

I love money and money loves me.

I now release the gold-mine within me. I am linked with an endless golden stream of prosperity which comes to me under grace in perfect ways.

Goodness and mercy shall follow me all the days of my life, and I shall dwell in the house of abundance forever.

<hr>

My God is a God of plenty, and I now receive all that I desire or require, and more.

<hr>

My supply is endless, inexhaustible, and immediate and comes to me under grace in perfect ways.

<hr>

All channels are free and all doors fly open for my immediate and endless, Divinely Designed supply.

<hr>

I give thanks that the millions which are mine by Divine Right, now pour in and pile up under grace in perfect ways.

<hr>

Unexpected doors fly open, unexpected channels are free, and endless avalanches of abundance are poured out upon me, under grace in perfect ways.

<hr>

I am fearless in letting money go out, knowing God is my immediate and endless supply.

<hr>

Infinite Spirit, open the way for my immediate supply, let all that is mine by Divine right now reach me, in great avalanches of abundance.

<hr>

I have a magical work in a magical way, I give magical service for magical pay.

<hr>

God is my unfailing supply, and large sums of money come to me quickly, under grace, in perfect ways.

For Debt

I deny debt; there is no debt in Divine Mind, no man owes me anything, all is squared. I send forth love and forgiveness.

◇◇◇◇◇◇◇

For Good Health

Florence states that "when man is harmonious and happy he is healthy! [...] Resentment, ill-will, hate, fear etc., etc., tear down the cells and poison the blood." (*Your Word Is Your Wand*)

Below you will find affirmations regarding different body parts and the emotional ailments that she metaphorically associates with them. For example, if you are having problems with your eyesight, then perhaps you are looking ahead to the future and seeing unhappy events ahead of you.

I deny fatigue, for there is nothing to tire me. I live in the Kingdom of eternal joy and absorbing interests. My body is "the body electric," timeless and tireless, birthless and deathless.

◇◇◇◇◇◇◇

Eternal gifts fill me:

Eternal Joy.

Eternal Youth.

Eternal Wealth.

Eternal Health.

Eternal Love.

Eternal Life.

⁂

I am a Spiritual Being—my body is perfect, made in
His likeness and image. The Light now streams through
every cell. I give thanks for my radiant health.

⁂

I am nourished by the Spirit within. Every cell in my body is filled
with light. I give thanks for radiant health and endless happiness.

⁂

Divine Love floods my consciousness with health,
and every cell in my body is filled with light.

⁂

Regarding Eyes

Fear, suspicion, seeing obstacles. These affirmations combat
watching for unhappy events to come to pass, living in the
past or future—not living in the now.

The Light of the Christ now floods my eyeballs. I have
the crystal clear vision of the Spirit. I see clearly and
distinctly there are no obstacles on my pathway. I
see clearly the fulfillment of my heart's desire.

⁂

I have the X-ray eyes of the Spirit, I see through apparent
obstacles. I see clearly the miracles come to pass.

⁂

I give thanks for my perfect sight. I see God in
every face, I see good in every situation.

⁂

I have the crystal clear vision of the Spirit. I look up and down and all around, for my good comes from North, South, East, and West.

My eyes are God's eyes, perfect and flawless. The Light of the Christ floods my eyeballs and streams on my pathway. I see clearly there are no lions on my way, only angels and endless blessings.

My eyes are God's eyes, I see with the eyes of spirit. I see clearly the open way; there are no obstacles on my pathway. I see clearly the perfect plan.

Regarding Ears

Ears are associated with strong personal will, stubbornness, and a desire not to hear certain things.

My ears are the ears of the Spirit. The Light of Christ now streams through my ears, dissolving all hardness or malformation. I hear clearly the voice of intuition and give instant obedience. I hear clearly glad tidings of great joy.

My ears are God's ears, I hear with the ears of the Spirit. I am nonresistant and am willing to be led.

Regarding Rheumatism

Rheumatism is said to be associated with fault finding and criticism.

The Light of the Christ now floods my consciousness,
dissolving all acidic thoughts.

I give thanks for my radiant health and happiness.

Regarding False Growths

Unwanted bodily growths can be associated with feelings of jealousy, hatred, resentment, and fear.

Every plant my Father in Heaven has not planted shall be rooted up. All false ideas in my consciousness are now obliterated. The light of the Christ streams through every cell, and I give thanks for my radiant health and happiness now and forevermore.

Regarding Heart Disease

Problems with your heart can be associated with fear, anger, and other emotions that can raise one's blood pressure.

My heart is a perfect idea in Divine Mind and is
now in its right place, doing its right work.

I have a happy heart, a fearless heart, and a loving heart.

The Light of the Christ streams through every cell,
and I give thanks for my radiant health.

Regarding Memory Loss

There is no loss of memory in Divine Mind, therefore, I recollect
everything I should remember and I forget all that is not for my good.

For Happiness

I am now deluged with the happiness that was planned for me in
the Beginning. My barns are full, my cup flows over with joy.

Happy surprises come to me each day.

I am harmonious, happy, and radiant. I am
detached from the tyranny of fear.

My happiness is built upon a rock. Happiness
is mine now and for all eternity.

My happiness is God's affair, therefore, no one can interfere.

As I am one with God, I am now one with my heart's desire.

I give thanks for my permanent happiness, my permanent
health, my permanent wealth, my permanent love.

I am harmonious, happy, and Divinely magnetic,
and now draw to me my ships over a calm sea.

God's ideas for me are perfect and permanent.

My heart's desire is a perfect idea in Divine Mine, incorruptible and indestructible, and now comes to pass, under grace in a magical way.

I am grateful that everything is working out exactly as it should.

For Guidance

I am always under direct inspiration. I know just what to do and give instant obedience to my intuitive leads.

All power is given unto me to be meek and lowly of heart. I am willing to come last, therefore, I come first.

I am Divinely sensitive to my intuitive leads and give instant obedience to what it tells me.

For Forgiveness

I forgive everyone, and everyone forgives me. The gates swing open for my good.

I call on the Law of Forgiveness. I am free from mistakes and the consequences of mistakes. I am under grace and not under karmic law.

For Faith

Adverse appearances work for my good, for God utilizes every
person and every situation to bring to me my heart's desire.

As the needle in the compass is true to the north, what
is rightfully mine is true to me. I am the North!

I am linked by an invisible, unbreakable magnetic cord
with all that belongs to me by Divine Right!

Thy Kingdom is come, Thy will is done in me and my affairs.

Every plan my Father in heaven has not planned is dissolved and
obliterated, and the Divine Design of my life now comes to pass.

What God has given me can never be taken
from me for His gifts are for all eternity.

I am poised and powerful, my greatest expectations
are realized in a miraculous way.

I water my wilderness with faith and suddenly it blossoms like a rose.

I now exercise my fearless faith in three ways—by
thinking, speaking, and acting. I am unmoved by
appearances, therefore appearances move.

I stand steadfast and strong, immovable. I give thanks
for my seeming impossible good to come to pass, for
I know, with God, accomplishment is easy.

What was mine in the beginning, is mine
now and always will be mine.

⸻

I know there is nothing to defeat God, therefore,
there is nothing to defeat me.

⸻

I wait patiently, I trust in the Universe. Evildoers cannot harm
me and the Universe now gives me my heart's desires.

⸻

I have fearless faith in the Universe's blessings. As I
approach, barriers vanish and obstacles disappear.

⸻

I am in perfect harmony with the working of the law,
for I know that Infinite Intelligence knows nothing of
obstacles, time, or space. It knows only completion.

⸻

God works in unexpected and magic ways His wonders to perform.

⸻

I am prepared for the fulfillment of my heart's desire.

⸻

I now dig my ditches deep with faith and understanding
and my heart's desire comes to pass in a surprising way.

⸻

My ditches will be filled at the right time, bringing
all that I have asked for, and more!

⸻

I put to rest my negative thoughts. They feed
on my fear but starve with my faith.

⸻

God's ideas cannot be moved, therefore, what is mine
by Divine Right will always be with me.

⸻

I give thanks that I now receive the righteous desires of my heart.

I have perfect confidence in the Universe and the
Universe has perfect confidence in me.

All things are easy and possible now.

I now stand aside and watch God work. It interests me to see how
quickly and easily He brings the desires of my heart to pass.

Before I called I was answered and I now gather
in my harvest in a remarkable way.

Seeming impossible doors now open to me.

My good is a perfect and permanent idea in Divine Mind,
and must manifest for there is nothing to prevent it.

I cast my burdens on the Christ within and live with peace in my soul.

As I am one with God, I am one with my good, for God is both the
Giver and the Gift. I cannot separate the Giver from the gift.

For Your Divine Plan

I let go of everything not divinely designed for me, and
the perfect plan of my life now comes to pass.

What is mine by Divine Right can never be taken from
me. God's perfect plan for me is built upon a rock.

I follow the magic path of intuition and know that it is right.

My mind, body, and affairs are now molded
according to the Divine Pattern within.

God is the only power, and that power is within me. There is
only one plan, God's plan, and that plan now comes to pass.

I give thanks that I now bring forth from the Universal Substance
everything that satisfies all the righteous desires of my heart.

I fill the place that I can fill and no one else can fill. I do
the things which I can do and no one else can do.

I am fully equipped for the Divine Plan of my life;
I am more than equal to the situation.

All doors now open for happy surprises, and the
Divine Plan of my life is sped up under grace.

Acknowledgments

My biggest, most sincere acknowledgment regarding this book is to the Law of Attraction, the Universe at large, and my editor Claire Sielaff at Ulysses Press, who contacted me out of the blue to determine my interest in writing this book on a topic I'm passionate about. I wanted to write more nonfiction books but was not certain about the subject, and the Universe provided an opportunity: the right opportunity. Thank you to Renee Rutledge, my copy editor, for questioning and polishing and pushing to make it the better book it became. With her help, I hope the words inside, both Florence's and my own, help people create the lives of their dreams.

Thank you to Chaille Bos, for being my best cheerleader and motivator. To my family, for their faith in my ability to conquer everything I put my mind to.

Thank you to Anita, Ang, Hannah, Imani, Jacob, Simon, Vince, and my parents, Hazell and Colin, for sharing their experiences with me and allowing me to tell their stories in this book so that their experiences might inspire or teach others.

Of course, thank you to Florence Scovel Shinn, for believing in herself and her message so strongly that, after receiving one too many rejections from publishers, she forged ahead and self-published *The Game of Life and How to Play It*, which has left a lasting impact and touched the lives of readers across the world.

The publication of her books is a true testament to the power of her faith in her Divine Plan. She trusted that her work had an audience and would make a positive difference. She ignored the obstacles in her way and found so much success independently that her legacy has continued even until now, eighty years after her death.

Finally, thank *you*, dear reader, for trusting me with your time. I hope some of what was discussed in these pages resonated with you. Changing your thoughts truly can change your life. It costs nothing, it requires no equipment, and there are no downsides to giving it a go.

About the Author

Sarah Billington is the publisher of Edwina Ray Stationery, a boutique company that offers a gorgeous collection of themed notebooks, health and well-being planners, goal-setting workbooks, coloring books, puzzle books, and more. She is also an author of young adult fiction and self-help nonfiction. When not crafting stories or creating interesting stationery to help you plan your best life, she can be found at home in Victoria, Australia, with good friends and her two cats.

Introduction

The laws of the Universe emerged from the New Thought philosophical movement of the nineteenth century. These philosophical concepts offer guidance to redirect your thoughts from negative aspects of your life (such as worries about the future, current stressors, and sources of anxiety) to the positives: cultivating gratitude for what you have, whether it be big or small, optimism, and a sense of anticipation that good things are coming.

With influences from ancient Greece, ancient Rome, Hinduism, Buddhism, Christianity, and other cultures and their related belief systems, the laws of the Universe focus on the relationship between thought, belief, and consciousness, and how you can harness them to create the life of your dreams.

In 1925, New Thought leader Florence Scovel Shinn discussed five laws in her books on metaphysical theory and affirmation: the Law of Prosperity (page 80), the Law of Karma (page 82), the Law of Forgiveness (page 90), the

Law of Nonresistance (page 92), and currently the most popular law of them all, the Law of Attraction (page 70).

Life has changed significantly since the days when Florence wrote her books, so as well as discussing the above laws and how to make them work for you, I have included several modern additions to contemplate in order to help you craft your dream life. These include the Law of Unwavering Desire (page 104), the Law of Delicate Balance (page 106), the Law of Harmony (page 106), and the Law of Universal Influence (page 109).

Ultimately, the philosophies discussed here encourage love, compassion, and forgiveness. They help you focus on your desires and will lead you to a more peaceful, happy life. Whether you believe wholeheartedly in the laws of the Universe or think they're a bit unconventional, there are very few downsides to investigating the fundamental principles and seeing how they can improve your life.

So why not try it?

What's Covered

In this book, I will discuss Florence Scovel Shinn, the New Thought movement, and metaphysical theory—the underpinning philosophy behind the laws and concepts Florence proposed for how to live your best life.